COYOTES
Last Animals on Earth?

COYOTES

Last Animals on Earth?

Harold E. Thomas

illustrated by LORENCE F. BJORKLUND

LOTHROP, LEE & SHEPARD COMPANY
NEW YORK

1 2 3 4 5 79 78 77 76 75

Library of Congress Cataloging in Publication Data

Thomas, Harold Edgell (date)
  Coyotes, last animals on earth?

  SUMMARY: Describes the characteristics and behavior of the coyote, including anecdotes from Indian lore and legend stressing its intelligence, and discussions of its importance to the environment.

  1. Coyotes—Juvenile literature.   [1. Coyotes]
I. Bjorklund, Lorence F., illus.   II. Title.
QL737.C22T48   599'.74442   74-26969
ISBN 0-688-41699-3
ISBN 0-688-51699-8 lib. bdg.

This book is dedicated to the Defenders of Wildlife and those other organizations which seek to protect the right of America's wildlife to live in our shared environment.

Acknowledgments

The author wishes to thank the following authors and publishers whose publications served as source material about Coyote in Indian myths and legends:

University of California Publications in American Archaeology and Ethnology:

"Coyote and Chicken Hawk," abridged from *Wappo Texts*, Vol. 19:1, by Paul Radin, 1924.

"Coyote and the Bullfish," abridged from *Wintu Myths*, Vol. 28:5, by Cora Du Bois and Dorothy Demetracopolou, 1931.

"Itsa and Isha Fight People," based on *Lovelock Cave*, Vol. 25:1, by Llewellyn L. Loud and M. R. Harrington, 1929.

The song "I Am Coyote" is from *More Mohave Myths* by A. L. Kroeber in *University of California Publications in Anthropological Records*, Vol. 27, 1972.

The Seri song "Coyote Is Happy in the Moonlight" is from *The Last of the Seris* by Dane and Mary Coolidge, Rio Grande Press edition, 1971. Quoted with permission of the Rio Grande Press, Inc.

Contents

1 · Dawn Coyote

Thousands of years ago on a hot, dry coastal plain where the city of Los Angeles now stands, a huge cat lay quietly, partially hidden by the leaves of an elderberry bush. It was just dawn and in the dim, hazy light the animal could see a herd of tiny four-horned antelope grazing far out on the grassy plain. Closer by, another enormous animal with coarse, shaggy fur and long, curving claws lumbered slowly toward a little pond surrounded by a grove of cypresses. The giant ground sloth grazed a moment, then raised his head to chew, revealing his massive chest and powerful forelegs. He took a few more awkward steps, then tore at the grass again.

High above him, perched on a dead limb of a cypress, the condor-like vulture sat waiting, holding his six-foot wings out from his body in an effort to cool himself. The huge vulture's image was dimly reflected on the still surface of the pond for a moment until the serenity of the water was broken by another bird entering the pool. The La Brea stork, four and a half feet tall, began wading in the turbid pond, probing the bottom with its cavernous bill.

As the ground sloth entered the grove, the cat, lacking the patience of its present-day descendants, began to growl, a low rumbling sound that startled the stork but did not deter the giant sloth from drinking. He had heard the sound before but his brain was not large enough to store many memories. The memory would have been a terrible one. His body, in spite of the bony armored plates imbedded in his thick skin, bore the scars of a previous encounter with a maker of such a sound.

But as the huge cat emerged from its hiding place, its voice rose to a hideous scream. The herd of little antelope, although a mile away, panicked and stampeded in all directions. A pack of dire wolves in the hills beyond the flat plains heard the terrifying sound and answered with challenging howls. The stork, frantically beating its enormous wings, sought safety in the trees. The giant sloth turned and half rose on his hind legs to meet the impact of the saber-toothed tiger's charge. Only the vulture did not stir.

The tiger came slowly, its slight hind legs not strong enough to give it the swiftness of the true cats. He screamed again and again as though to frighten his prey into submission, but the ponderous sloth, outweighing the cat several times over, stood his ground. The cat circled,

12

only snarling now as the sloth rose to its full height on its hind legs and clumsily turned to face its attacker. Suddenly the tiger, not having sufficient intelligence to be cautious, charged full against the massive chest of the giant sloth, rising up in an attempt to reach the ground sloth's throat.

The sloth swung his powerful forelegs around the tiger and began to crush the cat against his chest. For a moment the two behemoths seemed to be locked in an embrace as the tiger's claws sank into the sloth's armored back. But then the cat's two long, dagger-like teeth, curving down from its upper jaw, found their mark and the sloth soon lay still beside the pond.

The tiger, still snarling and growling, was just settling down to eat when the dire wolves arrived. There were twenty wolves, no four of them a match for the raking claws and dagger teeth of the great cat, although in large numbers they could subdue even the imperial mammoth. But their ponderous heads were provided with massive jaws and small brain cavities so that now only hunger penetrated their dim consciousnesses as they rushed to tear at the dead sloth.

The cat, roaring her rage, lunged at the entire pack of wolves, killing two of them with one swipe of her mighty paw. Half of the wolves turned to the attack, almost covering the screaming cat with their bodies as they slashed at her flanks and throat. But then, seeing some of their brothers beginning to feed on the carcass, they fell upon them with fury, slashing viciously at whatever was before their muzzles. The great saber-tooth, its hunger and fury overwhelming its pain, leaped into the midst of the snapping jaws.

13

Soon a new sound rose over the din of roars and howls at the pond—the sound of a thousand thunders rolling in the distance, near the shadow of the hills, as a great herd of *Bison antiquus* stampeded toward the pond.

Their titanic bodies, many seven feet tall, destroyed everything before them. Some bulls, with six-foot spread of horns, turned their heads in panic and pierced their neighbors' bodies, which then fell under the lacerating hoofs. For behind the herd came the most terrible predator of all—a tribe of men, whooping and screaming as they sought to thrust their spears in a bison's side.

On a little rise near the pond and overlooking the plains sat seven coyotes, waiting for the titans to finish their slaughter. Whether on the plains or by the pond mattered little to them. They would take what was left without risk and without any effort at all while the surviving great predators nursed their wounds or slept on their gorged bellies.

Dawn Coyote

Now the saber-toothed tiger and the giant ground sloth are long gone from the face of the earth. The *Bison antiquus* were modified by time into the smaller, almost hornless bison of today, themselves almost exterminated by latter-day tribes of white men. The dire wolves were perhaps ancestors of the present gray wolves, now relegated by humans to the northern parts of the continent. The stork is gone and perhaps time has molded the condor-like vulture into the present-day California condor. But humans have reduced their numbers to fewer than sixty birds. The tiny two-foot-high pronghorn antelopes no longer exist but their distant relatives, the much larger pronghorns of the Great Plains, are found in small numbers, only on this continent.

There were other beasts that shared the Age of Mammals with the coyote, such as the elephant-like mastodons and the enormous short-faced bear, the largest carnivore of the era, and even a strange short-faced coyote. And, too, there was the largest feline of all time, the great American lionlike cat, the progenitor of the modern jaguar which was last seen in California and most of the Southwest over one hundred years ago.

All those great beasts of the Age of Mammals have vanished or been greatly modified throughout eons of time, except the coyote. The modern coyote, *Canis latrans*, is little different from his ancient forebear, *Canis*

orcutti, whose bones were found in the La Brea tar pits in Los Angeles. The tar pits, which look deceptively like calm pools of water, have trapped countless unwary animals in their sticky depths over the centuries. Their bones, which we have extracted from the pits, have given us a record of those olden times.

It is not known, but is assumed by many, that human beings were present in that day. Human bones have never been found in the pits but people were undoubtedly too intelligent to be lured into them. The dire wolves and saber-toothed tigers are represented by the most skeletons, with coyotes being the third most often found. Even at that, coyote skeletons are outnumbered ten to one by those of the dire wolves. Although coyotes were probably more numerous, paleontologists have suggested that perhaps their greater intelligence helped most of them avoid the death traps.

As the big carnivores ripped and slashed one another into oblivion, the patient and canny coyote adapted to the dramatic alterations brought by the passing centuries with little change to his physical self. But it is no wonder. The Indians have said that all forms of life will pass through many worlds on this earth but there will be a final world in which all will perish but the coyote, doomed, some say, to roam the earth forever—the last animal on earth.

2 · In the Beginning Was Coyote

This is the Fifth World in which we all live, we animals and plants and rocks. Only Coyote, First Man, and First Woman came up out of the darkness of the First World so long ago. And in the worlds between, many things were created, some emerging into the next world, some remaining behind in the swirling, dimly glowing mists.

Many living things followed Coyote up the center of the soaring, hollow reed through the murky sky of the Fourth World into the Fifth. With him were the Holy People who shaped and sanctified the world they found. This, too, was so very long ago. But when this was done, they fell to quarreling and bickering among themselves. Coyote, although a dissenter himself and called Ahsteh-Hashkeh, the First-to-Be-Angry, because of his sharp tongue, was saddened by the arguments and anger.

He knew that Sun was at fault. Perhaps to amuse himself, Sun caused the rift among the Holy People. So Coyote went to see Sun and scolded him. "You are not setting a good example for the human beings yet to be created," Coyote said.

Sun was furious; his anger lit up the universe. He picked Coyote up with a streak of lightning and threw him against the flint wall of his hogan. Coyote hit so hard that some of his fur fell out. Sun picked him up again and threw him three more times against the flint walls. Each time some of Coyote's fur fell out. But he finally escaped from Sun's wrath and ran away to follow First Man.

Sun then picked up some of the fur. He blew it toward the east and white coyotes ran out. "You will live within the dawn," he told them. He blew some fur to the south and blue coyotes ran out. "You will live within the horizontal blue," he told them. He blew some fur to the west and yellow coyotes ran out. "You will live with the evening twilight," he told them. He blew some fur to the north and black coyotes ran out. "You will live within the darkness," he told them.

Sun blew the last bit of fur up into the air and many plain gray coyotes ran out. "You will roam the earth," he told them. "You will be thieves and you must run until exhausted before you can eat. You shall live according to the will of your chief." Their chief, of course, was Ahsteh-Hashkeh, First-to-Be-Angry.

The white invaders of the North American continent have probably never seen the white, blue, yellow, or black coyotes of the Navaho Indian origin stories. But they have seen thousands upon thousands of gray coyotes throughout the years since European explorers first traveled in the West. The Spanish conquistadores of Cortez's legions of greed and destruction knew of the coyote nearly three centuries before any English-speaking people made their acquaintance with the animal.

In 1804, William Clark, co-commander of the Lewis and Clark overland expedition to Oregon, saw a coyote, shot it, and made the first recorded report of the animal in English. A member of the party wrote that "the bones was taken apart and saved, as well as the skin—in order to send back to the States next Spring, with other Curiosities . . ."

At first Clark thought the animal was a fox but later he decided it was another species of wolf which he described as the "small or burrowing wolf of the prairie." Several years passed before it was realized that Clark's prairie wolf, the Aztec *coyote*, and the Spanish *coyotl* were all the same animal, but the name "prairie wolf" or "brush wolf" remained in use for a long time. Finally, three Anglo mispronunciations of the Spanish word gained favor and today we have a choice of "ki-oh'-tee," "ki'-yot," or "ki-yoht'."

A peculiar thing about the early reports of the coyote was that no one could decide whether the animals hunted singly, in small groups, or in packs. Clark wrote that they "associate in bands of ten or twelve, sometimes more," and are rarely found alone. Other travelers mentioned seeing coyotes in packs small and large. John James Audubon, the painter and naturalist, wrote in his journal about seeing singles and pairs, yet in his book on animals he described the coyotes as running in packs.

Records from Mexico going back to the sixteenth century refer to the coyote as generally ranging alone. Possibly prairie coyotes did run in packs while the Mexican coyotes did not. It is possible, too, that after the great buffalo slaughter began, which littered the plains with carrion, coyotes were observed in great numbers sharing the carcasses. Even today several coyotes may meet over a carrion dinner, but then they will go their separate ways. It would be easy to assume that coyotes that eat together hunt and live together, but today we know that they do not. We know that they are unsocial, highly territorial animals. A. Starker Leopold, one of the nation's leading wildlife authorities, writes that there is no evidence whatsoever that coyotes run in packs, despite claims to the contrary.

Perhaps most significant is that the Indian stories of most tribes scattered throughout the West refer to the coyote as a lonely wanderer. Most of the legends concern Coyote the god, the spirit, or the demigod—half human, half ethereal being residing on earth. But when the plain old coyote is mentioned, he is alone or with his mate.

Some said Coyote was the first animal. Some even said Coyote created the earth out of bits of mud, a feather or two, a few straws—out of whatever was available, he made a world for himself in which to roam.

Coyote himself was a symbol. To the majority of the Indians west of the Mississippi River he was a multiple character—the godlike Creator, the semi-godlike Transformer who molds or changes what has been created, and the very human Trickster who is mean and mischievous, wise and stupid, greedy and vain. Coyote was a holy and unholy trinity, all in one—the balance of good and evil that exist in all things, as the Navaho say.

20

The Indians saw Coyote as a divine being and an utter fool, a benefactor bringing gifts to mankind and a scheming scoundrel who lies and cheats—and in many cases all these things in one. There was hardly a tribe west of the Mississippi River, from the Shuswap in British Columbia to the Maya of the Yucatán Peninsula in southern Mexico, which did not venerate or ridicule Coyote in some way, or thank him or condemn him for the way things are in life.

The aspects of his character ranged from that of a mischievous rascal with a sense of humor like that of the Indians to the great god Huehuecoyotl of the Aztecs or the god of the Nahuas of Mexico who erected a temple in his honor with an elite corps of priests devoted to his service, carved his statue in stone, and built an enormous tomb for him when he died.

As Creator, Coyote was arrogant and sometimes even deceitful so that he could be certain that things would be made the way he wanted them. He was sometimes wise but often made mistakes with his creations and had to do them over. He created human beings in various ways, depending upon the tribe that told the story. We were made, like the earth itself, out of bits of straw or mud, a few feathers stuck in the ground, or flotsam and jetsam washed upon the beaches, or the innards of water monsters slain by Coyote himself.

Coyote usually created people in a whimsical, offhand manner as though he needed something to do—something with which to amuse himself. The Wappo, who once lived in the beautiful Napa Valley of northern California, said that the world was once all water except for some mountaintops where Coyote and his grandson, Chicken-hawk, lived. But then the waters rose and the two beings were saved only after they locked themselves in a rock. When

21

the waters receded, Coyote came out of his rock and looked around. There was nobody there.

"Well, what are we going to do, Grandfather?" asked Chicken-hawk.

"We'll make some people," said Coyote and he immediately built a sweathouse. Then he picked up some feathers and stuck them in the ground.

"Well," he said to the feathers, "you shall become people." And they did.

But the next morning the people just lay on the ground in the sweathouse. They did not move or speak.

"Grandfather," said Chicken-hawk, "what is the matter with them? They don't talk."

So Coyote took a sack and went to see old man Moon.

"I have come for a bag of words," he told the Moon, and the old man filled the sack with words and tied up the end. When Coyote returned to the sweathouse and opened the sack, the people started speaking.

But the next morning when everybody woke up Chicken-hawk said, "Grandfather! The people are not moving." So Coyote took his sack and went to old man Moon again.

"I have come for a bag of fleas," he told Moon, and the sack was filled with fleas. When Coyote returned to the sweathouse and opened the sack, the fleas jumped out and bit the people. They began to move about.

But the next morning when all awoke, Chicken-hawk said, "Grandfather, there's something wrong with the people. They don't laugh."

So Coyote again took his sack to old man Moon. "I have come for a bag of laughter." So Moon filled the sack with laughter and Coyote returned to the sweathouse. He opened the sack and the people began to laugh.

But the next morning Chicken-hawk said, "Grand-father, there's something wrong. The people don't eat."

So Coyote took his sack to old man Moon and said, "I have come for a bag of pinole, bread, and acorn mush."

When Coyote returned and opened the sack, all the people ate.

They all stayed there and were very happy.

As the Transformer, Coyote molded and battered the earth into its present shape, arranged the planets in the sky, set the sun on its proper course and even became the sun when necessary, added some moons when there were too few and destroyed moons when there were too many. Since he knew all things, he transformed the minds of human beings by giving them knowledge.

Perhaps the greatest transformation Coyote brought to the earth was death. It did not take him long to see that all the living things would multiply and overrun the earth. The people did not like to die but had no choice other than to submit to Coyote's superior wisdom. But sometimes they would seek revenge and cause the death of one of his kin. In spite of all his power, Coyote could do nothing to bring back even his own child from the death he himself had brought upon the earth.

The third aspect of Coyote, that of the Trickster, is the one that probably has inspired the greatest number of tales. They are the ones the Indian storytellers must have liked to tell best. A number of tribes had whole cycles of Coyote Trickster stories. In most of them Coyote is not invested with any religious or supernatural implication. He is a very human-like Trickster—foolish, vain, mischievous, and just plain stupid.

More often than not it was Coyote who was out-tricked,

often in revenge for some practical joke he had played. Among the Winnebago Indians of Wisconsin, Wakdjunkaga was the trickster figure. He delighted in getting the best of Coyote who, of course, was well known for his cleverness. One day Wakdjunkaga decided to play on Coyote's enormous ego. He put a horse to sleep and asked Mouse to tell Coyote that there was a dead horse that should be moved away from the village. Only too glad to be part of the hoax, Mouse went to Coyote and told him about the horse. He said, "I know you are very strong and will be able to pull the horse away." Coyote agreed that he was very strong and went with Mouse to where the horse was lying. Mouse tied the horse and Coyote together by their tails.

Coyote started to pull. The horse woke up and began racing in fright about the village with Coyote bouncing up and down behind him. Wakdjunkaga called for everybody in the village to come see what the foolish Coyote was doing. The horse finally went to its master and Coyote was untied. He just sat there, his mouth twitching in shame. He left the village and has never lived with people since then.

Since the day of Ahsteh-Hashkeh, the plain gray coyotes that Sun decreed should roam the earth have been doing just that. Once their range was from the Pacific Ocean to the Mississippi River and from British Columbia to southern Mexico. Now they have been sighted as far north as Point Barrow, Alaska, and as far south as Costa Rica in Central America. And they are moving east. Long found in the provinces of British Columbia and Alberta, they were sighted in Ontario in 1919 and in Quebec in 1952 and finally were found in New Brunswick in 1958. Most recently they have moved into suburban Toronto and at night spread quietly throughout the city.

In the eastern United States they seem to be increasing, especially in New Hampshire and Vermont and in the Adirondacks in New York. At one time or another they have been seen in every state in the union except Delaware and Hawaii, but most of those sighted in the South and Southeast were pets that had escaped or were released. Coyotes seem to prefer country that is either hot and dry or cool and moist, so the states with muggy weather will probably have to do without them.

But as far as the other states, provinces, and countries in North and Central America are concerned, sooner or later the coyotes will be there if they aren't already. And they will be singing their song in the night. If you hear it, perhaps it will be the song of the "coyote who owns the morning," heard often at dawn by the Mohave Indians who live near the Colorado River in California.

I am Coyote.
I know everything
but I have no home.
I run across the desert
and I have no road.
Yet I live all right.

3 · Song of the Coyote

The desert of the Southwest is quiet tonight. No night insects buzz. There is no breeze to whine among the rocks. No animals scurry across the still, hot sands. The moon has just risen from behind a distant mesa and long shafts of shadows strike across the desert floor. Mesas and pinnacles silhouetted in the east are seen as fantastic and grotesque forms—gargoyles, monsters frozen in stone. It is as if in this place all life has ceased to exist.

But suddenly an eerie cry is heard, a lonely wail trembling in the night air. The strange sound echoes from the walls and caverns of the mesas. No sooner has the cry begun than it is answered from another direction and then from yet another. Next it comes from the tall pinnacle to the north, then from close by, and the whole desert valley is filled with the sound. Just as suddenly, as if by signal, the sound stops. And all is still in the desert as before.

Song of the Coyote

The same cry might very well be heard in the mountains of California or Colorado, in the vast rolling expanses of the Great Plains, in the great forests of British Columbia, or in the tropical jungles of Guatemala or Costa Rica. It is the cry of the coyote—a song of the wilderness. After the noise of the city, the deafening roar of jet airplanes, the eternal rumble of automobiles, or just the hubbub of human voices, the call of the coyote is indeed a welcome sound, reminding us that there is still wildness to be experienced.

In our desert scene we may hear the cry again and again or we may hear nothing at all for the rest of the night. But the memory of the sound does not leave us. It is too haunting, too lively to be forgotten. It may have been only one or two coyotes or it may have been many. A single coyote can somehow make himself sound like a pair and two can sound like several. He is thought by some to be able to throw his voice to make it seem as though it is coming from somewhere besides where he is actually howling.

Whatever method the coyote uses to produce his uncanny sounds, his is one of the most impressive voices to be heard in the North American wilds. It is unlike the voice of his canine cousins, the dog and the wolf. Only two of the eight canine species of the world can even approach the coyote in the rich variety of sounds he is capable of making. These are the golden jackal and black-backed jackal of the Old World. The gray wolf and the dog generally have the same vocal patterns, although the wolf is noted more for its mournful howl and the dog, of course, for its barking. The coyote does bark but seldom seems able to satisfy himself with so simple a sound, and follows a few throat-clearing barks with a torrent of seemingly hysterical yips mingled with wailing notes, all voiced so quickly that it sounds as if he is barking and howling simultaneously. Nor does he seem capable of sustaining a nice mellow howl without letting his enthusiasm for a rich assortment of notes get the best of him. In other words, he cannot communicate with a simple statement—he must sing a song. For that reason he is often called the Song Dog.

The Paiutes of the Great Basin deserts knew that Coyote was the father of songs. They knew, too, that every man had to have his song or he would have no power and could not pray to the spirits nor even please his own people. The Paiutes say that in olden times there was such a man who had no song and that his name was Sinoauv. During clan gatherings he sat apart from everyone, too sad and ashamed to mingle with the others without a song to sing to them.

But one day while Sinoauv was gathering tule roots to eat, Coyote himself came by. Naturally he was hungry, so he bargained for some of the roots. Sinoauv asked for a song—a song that would please the hearts and stir the thoughts of his people. Becoming very daring, he asked for a coyote song.

At first Coyote offered a rich song that would gain him favor with the spirits. But Sinoauv, noticing how thin Coyote was, insisted he would take only a coyote song in exchange for the juicy roots. Finally Coyote's hunger won out and he gave the young man a coyote song with the understanding that it would be used only to please his people and stir their thoughts.

It was at the time of harvesting the pinyon pine nuts when all the clans gathered together that Sinoauv first sang the song Coyote had given him. The people were

very happy to hear the song and said to each other that it was so sweet it surely must be a coyote song.

The people asked him to sing the song again and again. The more he sang it the more pleased he was with the sound of his voice and the praises of the people. Before long he began to change the words little by little until the people began to say he sang the song of Sinoauv, not Coyote. So that night, when Sinoauv lay sleeping, exhausted from so much singing and pride, Coyote crept into camp and took back his song.

Now, even today, Sinoauv has no song—only a lonely

howl that can sometimes be heard in the northern woods. For Sinoauv is the Paiute name for wolf.

As if to lend credibility to that legend, biologists studying some canines which they simply called "New Hampshire canids," since they were not certain what the animals were, noted that their charges vocalized only a few times a day and then only briefly. Then, a few months after some coyotes were brought in from Colorado, the mysterious canids began to sing more like the coyotes and up to fifteen times a day. But when the coyotes were removed, the canids went back to their old patterns of expression and again only a few times a day.

Not all Indians thought so highly of the coyote's voice as did the Paiutes. In the creation story of the Yuma Indians, who live along the lower part of the Colorado River, when the spirits called upon the people to sing Coyote insisted on leading. But when he sang, such foolish wails came out of his mouth that the people could bear no more and drove him away.

When two or more coyotes join in unison, it is like an off-key concert where each musician sings whatever comes into his head. To someone fresh from the city, the sound is often frightening or at least it is enough to cause one's skin to tingle from dread. But to those who know and love the wilderness, it is one of the beautiful songs of nature.

Hearing a coyote chorus for the first or hundredth time, one may wonder why they sing and what they are saying. Some scientists who look for the practical reason for everything claim that an animal vocalizes only as a response to the pressures of hunger, fear, sex drives, territoriality, and so on. Perhaps such scientists speak for themselves, but no one is knowledgeable enough to deny

32

that animals have emotions and can express happiness and sorrow, can appreciate a pleasant environment, and do things simply for pleasure. Who is to say a coyote does not sing to vent exuberance and joy at being alive?

One may speculate at length concerning the reasons coyotes yip and howl. Obviously it is also one way in which they communicate. Certain varying combinations of barks, yips, yaps, wails, squeals, howls, and even snorts, mysterious to us, could be signals, warnings of danger, calls for help or even requests for information.

Since coyotes are thought to mate for life and the pups usually stay with the parents until they are several months old, it is reasonable to expect a coyote to howl in order to discover the whereabouts of its mate or pup. Or perhaps a solitary coyote's sad song from some hilltop may be to express his loneliness, to call another coyote to his side, or simply to ask for reassurance that another coyote is there somewhere in the wilderness.

It is common for coyotes to howl at each other while long distances apart and then go on about their business with no intention of meeting. At times that lonesome voice may start a coyote choir singing. Even a sudden loud noise may strike the right note to start up their choir. Tame coyotes respond to musical instruments and will join the human family in an evening of song. In captivity, coyotes will even join wolves or other canines for a concert.

We can only wonder what the coyotes are singing, but the Indians understood the songs. Many of their chants were modeled after the animal's howls and yips. Among the Cheyenne Indians of the Great Plains a certain few had a strange power. They could talk with coyotes, or at least understand the animal's singing. These special persons were much respected and no one doubted them when

they translated from the coyote.

George Bird Grinnell, who lived with and wrote about the Cheyenne almost a hundred years ago, tells of a war party of Cheyenne Fox soldiers, one of the warrior societies, on their way to the country of the Ute Indians. They had asked a man named Dives Backward to go with them because they knew of his ability to understand the talk of coyotes. One night at camp they heard a coyote bark. Two Buttes, the chief, asked Dives Backward what the little wolf had said and he told the chief that it was bad—the coyote had said that one of the party would be killed if they did not change their direction of travel.

When the chief announced this to the party, Sun Maker, another of the war leaders, scoffed and said they should not be frightened at everything they heard and saw. But the next morning Two Buttes and forty of his warriors accepted the warning of the coyote and turned back for home. Sun Maker and twenty braves stayed where they were. Later, one of them was killed by a Ute as the coyote had predicted.

The Seri Indians of Tiburón Island in the Gulf of California did not talk to coyotes but they felt a kinship with the animal. Their country was very harsh and barren and there was not much food for either coyote or Indian. The Seri understood the coyote's howl when they sang this song about him:

> The coyote is happy in the moonlight.
> He sings a song to the moon
> while he dances.
> And he jumps far away,
> while he dances.
> When the coyote is very happy
> he sings his song
> with his nose to the ground,
> running round and round.

4 · Dinner and
Dinner Guests

The summer sun had just disappeared behind a ridge but dusk did not cool the hot, dry foothills of the Sierra Nevada Mountains of California. The warm breeze that had swept up out of the San Joaquin Valley during the afternoon had stopped with the setting of the sun and now all was still except for the clanging of cowbells in the distance and the chortling whistle of an ash-throated flycatcher.

A group of turkey vultures swirled overhead in descending spirals until they alighted to roost in tall, twisted digger pines silhouetted against the pale red light of the western horizon. In the east, rolling pink thunderheads loomed over the still snowy peaks of the Sierra divide.

36

Near by, a ground squirrel scampered onto the top of a granite boulder. He sat up on his haunches and, with a voice like a rusty wheel, squeaked at the evening landscape. A badger appeared from a clump of manzanita bushes and the ground squirrel quickly disappeared into his hole at the base of the boulder.

As the badger waddled toward the hole on his short legs, a coyote came out from the bushes and nipped at the badger's rump. The badger turned around and growled once at the coyote, then again started for the hole. The coyote ran ahead of the badger, sniffed around the hole and ran back to the badger as though to hurry him. But he was not one to be rushed.

The badger finally reached the hole and began digging. The coyote watched him for a while and then sniffed about the boulder until he found the squirrel's escape hole on the other side of the rock. There he crouched to wait. The badger continued with his work methodically, scratching the dirt underneath him with the long claws of his front paws and simultaneously shoving the dirt away with his hind paws.

The badger may be slow-gaited but he is one of the world's fastest diggers, so it was not long until the badger completely disappeared into the enlarged hole. It was also not long before the squirrel decided he'd better use his

escape hole. When he did, the coyote had instant dinner. The indomitable badger dug a little further until he recognized that his prey had escaped into his friend's mouth. Then he backed out of the hole and waddled away, with the coyote and his full stomach following contentedly behind him.

This kind of hunting partnership between coyotes and badgers has been observed often. The coyote is not by any means always the benefactor of the arrangement. Most times the badger gets to his meal before the rodent manages to escape, and the coyote goes hungry for a while longer. A badger may follow a coyote who has chased a rabbit into a hole and wait patiently until the coyote gives up digging, which is usually very quickly. Then the badger, with his superior digging ability, will take over the job and get the reward.

The cynical might assume that when a coyote and a badger become partners the extent of their relationship is simply the opportunistic use of each other's talents to obtain food. But an incident reported in South Dakota some years back could be taken as an indication that the bond between the two very dissimilar animals is much stronger. The observer noticed a coyote sitting near a railroad bank intently watching something under some bushes. Looking through his binoculars, the man saw a badger excitedly sniffing through the brush. The coyote moved occasionally to stay close to the badger. When the smaller animal finally gave up his search, the two of them climbed the embankment and trotted off down the railroad tracks side by side "like a couple of hoboes," as the observer put it. It must have been quite a sight to see the short-legged, squat little animal waddling on down the tracks with his tall, skinny friend.

The world of the coyote and the badger has been so disturbed that the full significance of their relationship may remain a mystery because there are so few, if any, places left where animals can still be observed in their natural condition. The ancient Indians of Mexico, such as the Aztecs, seemed to recognize a bond between the two animals. Their name for the badger was *Tlalcoyotl*, meaning "coyote of the earth." Many more northern tribes sang songs and told stories of the brothers Coyote and Badger.

One may wonder why the coyote does not consider the badger as a prospective dinner rather than as a partner. A good reason is the badger's ferocity which, like most other members of the weasel family, gives him fighting ability and courage enough to give even a cougar second thoughts. Another reason is his loose skin and thick fur which make it almost impossible for any enemy to get a grip on him. The badger also has a concealed weapon he may use in times of danger. Like his cousin, the skunk, he has a musk gland under his tail from which he can discharge a strong, repelling scent. But, unlike the skunk, he depends more on his teeth, claws, and nasty disposition.

An important part of the coyote's amazing ability to adapt to circumstances is his craftiness in using animals of other species to help him obtain food. The coyote simply takes advantage of their feeding habits to benefit himself and he enters into a partnership of sorts with them whether they like it or not.

As an example, a coyote may use large, hoofed animals as his "beaters." Some of the coyotes of colder climates follow behind moose or elk in the winter snow. As the larger animal paws through the snow looking for grass or herbs, mice are frightened out of hiding and into the coyote's clutches. Coyotes also have often been seen in meadows and pastures with herds of cattle, seemingly grazing right along with them. But again the coyotes are taking advantage of the big animals' disturbance of mouse runs.

The coyote's opportunism is not limited to other mammals. Birds are often his helpmates. In the deserts, valleys, and especially in the brushy foothills of the West one can usually see turkey vultures circling overhead or riding the air currents. These huge birds may be just enjoying themselves but more often they are searching the earth below for food and watching each other to see which bird will soar downward, indicating that a meal has been spotted. If you were a quiet and patient observer in the high plains of eastern Oregon (part of the Great American Desert), and if you watched the vultures long enough, you might see an interesting example of how the coyote benefits from the habits of other animals.

The vultures have been spiraling in the bright afternoon sky for an hour, making their slow and graceful turns after each other as though playing a lazy game of tag. Then one bird leaves the cone of vultures and heads straight to the north, never flapping his wings but simply gliding with the air. Soon he begins to circle again, but with each arc he descends a little until finally he is but a hundred feet or so over the brush.

He has spied a dead steer and is now circling the carcass, looking about to see if it is safe to land. Soon his companions catch up and swirl overhead in a much tighter circle than before. Then they too begin to descend.

Unknown to the birds, a coyote has been concealed in the brush a few hundred yards away. He has been alternately gnawing on an old and not very nutritious antelope bone and watching the vultures. When he sees the one bird descending, he knows a meal is near by. He drops the bone and trots through the brush toward the vultures.

He comes upon the steer's carcass just after the first of the birds have landed. he dashes at them, yipping and snapping. The birds take off with much flapping and hissing, but one vulture is too slow and is trapped by the coyote. The bird promptly throws up the vile-smelling contents of its stomach, which is one of the ways in which a turkey vulture protects itself, and falls over, seemingly unconscious.

But the coyote is not interested in a vulture dinner; he turns and begins tearing hungrily at the carcass. A pair of crows and a black-billed magpie who, in turn, had been watching the coyote and had followed him to the scene, station themselves in the brush. They flash in now and then to snatch up morsels missed by the coyote. The vultures continue spiraling overhead, waiting for the coyote to gorge himself and leave. The lone vulture left on the ground recovers from its fright and takes off in the lumbering, awkward fashion of its kind.

Suddenly the small birds set up a clamor of squawking from the bushes. The coyote, alerted, stops feeding and sniffs the air. He sees that the vultures have moved higher in their circling. He turns, sniffs again, catches a dreaded scent and trots away into the brush. Not long afterward a rancher on horseback, who has been watching the vultures, finds his missing steer.

The coyote is not the only one that benefits from his relationship with birds. Vultures also watch coyotes at the hunt. They anticipate a kill and hover about, hoping to pick up a snack after the coyotes are finished. Crows, ravens, magpies and other winged carrion eaters often follow a coyote about with the intention of sharing his meal. And, as if in payment, they serve him as lookouts.

Coyotes, more than all other North American mammals except humans, seem to learn new ways to collaborate with one another. They watch each other to learn new tricks of the hunt, or more often join in a hunting venture and learn by participating with a coyote that already has a new way to obtain food.

One of the commonest systems of cooperative hunting used by coyotes is the relay tactic. This is used to run down animals that can run faster than they can, such as jackrabbits and pronghorn antelopes. Unluckily for those animals, they have a tendency to circle when they are pursued and coyotes take advantage of this fact. For example, a pair of coyotes may spot a herd of pronghorns and give chase. The coyotes will shortly determine which one of the herd is the slowest, and therefore probably the weakest, and concentrate on it.

When the pronghorn begins to circle, one of the coyotes will drop out of the chase, take a short cut across the diameter of the circular path he knows the pronghorn will make, and conceal himself behind a bush or rock. He waits for the pronghorn to pass and then immediately takes up the chase again. At this point the other coyote stops to take a rest. The coyotes continue trading off while slowly forcing the pronghorn to run in a tighter circle until it finally tires and becomes easy prey for the canines.

A peculiarity in pronghorn behavior will sometimes net a pair of coyotes a meal. Pronghorns, unlike deer, will not jump over fences, although they are perfectly capable of doing so. Wise coyotes in the plains have learned this and will sometimes run a pronghorn up against a fence and trap it. Of course at that point the animal may well turn and fight, so the coyotes' cleverness may net them nothing but sore hides.

The pronghorn is, however, an easy prey only if it has been weakened by disease or malnutrition or parasites. Otherwise the coyotes may be overmatched in facing the sharp hoofs and horns. Pronghorns have been known to cut down a coyote with their sharp front hoofs. One report from the Great Plains described eight pronghorns chasing a single coyote before he finally tried to hide in a bush. The angry animals trampled the bush and the coyote to pieces and one pronghorn hooked the coyote's carcass into the air with its horns.

Pronghorn antelopes are more often called by the latter name than the former, but they are not antelopes. They have no close relations anywhere in the world and are an animal family unto themselves. They have horns rather than antlers, and are the only mammals in the world that shed them each year. They, like the coyote, are part of our unique wildlife heritage, found only on this continent. They are estimated to have numbered over 100,000,000 when they were roaming the plains with the bison, until the white man slaughtered both almost to extinction.

Now, through careful management, the pronghorn herds have been built back up. Today there are almost a

half million pronghorns in the United States, Canada, and Mexico. Some wildlife authorities complain that coyotes in some areas prey on pronghorn to such an extent that the herds are endangered. But other experts claim that coyotes have little effect on the herds. Most agree, however, that coyotes do have more effect on pronghorn than on deer.

Even though it was through man's management that the pronghorn numbers have increased, man, not the coyote, is still the pronghorn's greatest enemy. As an example, there was once a desert subspecies of the animal. Antelope Valley, a desert area near Los Angeles, was named after them. Years ago, when the railroad was put through the valley, the pronghorn starved to death because they would not cross the tracks to migrate for food.

In the 1940s there was one herd of desert pronghorn left. Military personnel during World War II wiped out the herd for fun and frolic. The coyote may be able to take one pronghorn now and then, but only man can destroy an entire herd.

Acting crazy will often get coyotes their dinner. One coyote, while still some distance away from the intended prey, will suddenly seem to go mad. He may leap into the air for no reason, snatch up pieces of wood and throw them into the air, stagger around, perhaps chase his tail and run around in circles. In the meantime, coyote number two will sneak through the brush until he gets close enough to pounce on the animal that has been fascinated by the antics of the first coyote.

Of North American canids only the coyote, the gray wolf, and the red fox practice this trick, called "fascination display" by wildlife scientists. It has not been reported, however, that the wolf and the red fox use a partner.

A variation on that maneuver is the "double rush," where two coyotes run into a prairie dog town wildly yapping and snapping right and left. The idea seems to be to confuse the dogs into scampering helter-skelter all over their town. The big rodents range away from their territories within the town and may hesitate before ducking into a burrow in a territory not their own. This hesitation may be their undoing. There have also been reports of coyotes and badgers pairing up to do the "double rush" in a dog town.

There are times when the coyote's acts of cooperation border on the ingenious. Ernest Thompson Seton, the well-known naturalist and writer, seventy years ago wrote of how coyotes work together in the prairie dog country of the Great Plains. The prairie dog is not a dog, of course, but a burrowing rodent that emits a bark-like cry.

In this trick, two coyotes trot straight toward a dog while it is still squatting at the mounded entrance to its burrow. One of the coyotes walks directly behind the leader, keeping down as much as possible to avoid being seen by the dog. When the lead coyote gets close enough to threaten the dog, the rodent disappears into his hole. As he does, the coyote jumps directly over the hole and continues on his way as though he were not at all interested in prairie dogs. Meantime the second coyote immediately stops and crouches down.

Prairie dogs have a habit which coyotes can count on. After an enemy passes by or over their hole, they immediately stick their heads back out of the hole, almost always looking only in the direction the attacker has taken. Needless to say, when the dog makes this mistake the second coyote makes the kill.

There are many stories similar to the ones we have told that relate how the coyote adapts to the environment of his particular locality. It is significant that he does not necessarily stick to unvarying hunting habits, as do most animals, but is able to take advantage of situations as they develop and to "think out" a plan when food is hard to get. Perhaps it is one of the most important reasons for his survival.

But of course it all depends on his location, what is available, and what is the most desirable and easiest to come by. Whatever coyotes are found to have been eating at the time of a study does not indicate that it is their normal prey. In fact, it would be safe to say that coyotes have no normal fare. One study of the stomach contents of

47

coyotes killed in a northern state showed that they had been subsisting solely on bear! Needless to say, it had to be carrion—the dead and decaying flesh from an old kill.

Not many studies would indicate salmon as a staple of coyote diet, yet along northwestern streams during the season when the big fish from the sea are battling up the raging streams to their spawning grounds, coyotes take advantage of those fish, too weak or too old to make the rugged journey, that drift helplessly near the banks, or those upstream which are exhausted from spawning.

But perhaps fish have gotten their revenge. According to the Wintu of California's Sacramento Valley, at least on one occasion a fish ate a coyote.

Coyote was going up the river to visit someone. He looked very fine. He had his quiver, bow and arrows, moccasins and beads. It was a hot summer day. He came to a nice stretch of sand. He saw Bullfish sunning himself. Coyote said, "What are you doing there?" Bullfish didn't say a word. Coyote talked and talked but Bullfish never answered.

At last Coyote said, "You are pretty small. You are too little to do anything. I bet you can't swallow my toe," and at the same time he thrust his toe in front of Bullfish's mouth. Bullfish just turned his head away. Then Coyote said, "I'll give you my bow and arrows if you bite me." He teased Bullfish that way for a long time.

Finally Bullfish nipped Coyote's toe. Coyote did not pay any attention to him; he only continued to taunt him. Soon Bullfish had swallowed Coyote's leg. Coyote became frightened and begged for mercy but Bullfish ignored him and kept on swallowing him. Coyote offered him all his fine things but Bullfish just swallowed him entirely and swam off under a rock in the riffle.

The people missed Coyote. They hunted for him and found his valuables on the sand and saw the track where he had been dragged in. So they asked a doctor to find out where he was. The doctor went into a trance and about the middle of the night said that he was under the water; Bullfish had swallowed him.

Then Bullfish made the water muddy so the people could not find him. At last Water Bird climbed a tree and looked. He said, "I see a tail under a rock in the riffle. I am going to try to spear him." So he took a spear pole, aimed carefully, and speared Bullfish right above the tail. The people pulled him out and cut open his abdomen. Coyote jumped out and said, "Nephew, I have been sleeping."

In the Big Horn Mountains of Wyoming, at least during part of the year, coyotes have been known to subsist almost entirely on marmots, or woodchucks as they are sometimes called. They are the largest rodents in North America and are noted for being very incautious. They love to stand up on their hind legs and survey the world, as do most of the ground squirrel family. Coyotes find it easy to make quick work of the clumsy, slow-moving animals.

Coyotes are well known for their penchant for fruit. They prowl orchards at night to pick up the fallen fruit, nibble berries off vines, and raid melon patches. This of course enrages the farmer. Wild fruits of all kinds are a delight to them and they will give up all semblance of a protein diet in favor of juicy, ripe fruit. Not too long ago it was thought that coyotes would eat fruit and grass only if no other food was available, but patient observers have found that they pass up easily obtainable rodents and even more easily obtainable carrion when fruit is in season.

A recent study on a wildlife refuge in Texas showed that

from early April to late May coyotes dined on a high percentage of wild fruits. Later in the summer they turned with relish to the wild persimmon and prickly pear cactus fruits. The Seri Indians of Mexico say they learned how to eat the cactus fruits by watching coyotes roll them along the ground to remove the thorns.

A study made in Yellowstone National Park at a time when coyotes had nominal protection showed mice and gophers to be the main fare for dinner. Elk, insects, birds, various rodents and rabbits, deer, bear, pronghorn, and bison served as side dishes in small quantities. The larger animals were probably consumed as carrion. It is certain that the bear were.

The study also showed that the coyote's taste for dessert varied widely. Listed were such "foods" as garbage, leather gloves, rags, strings, banana peels, orange and lemon rinds, a rivet, cellophane, seven inches of curtain, eight inches of rope, rubber, tinfoil, shoestrings and a piece of gunnysack. A diet like that corroborates the saying that "a coyote will eat anything that doesn't eat him first."

According to old frontier stories, coyotes will also eat humans—dead ones, of course. In fact, the Seri Indians of Mexico say that Coyote created death so that he would have bodies to eat. There have been no indications, either from old Indian or pioneer tales, that coyotes have ever attacked a living human, even if wounded and disabled. Coyotes are known for their patience.

Men have been known to eat coyotes. All western Indian tribes had a taboo against eating or often even killing a coyote. Depending on the tribe, the coyote was either too sacred, too powerful, or too evil to serve as food. Many of the tribes did eat dogs. They kept many of them around

camp for that purpose when elk, deer, and bison were hard to find.

But Lewis and Clark, while on their great exploration to the Northwest, had a coyote dinner at least one time during a particularly cruel winter in 1805. They had eaten dog with the Indians before and didn't see much difference.

Adolph Murie in Yellowstone National Park reported many indications that coyotes wait for elk to die of disease or starvation rather than kill them. Elk, unlike most of the deer family as well as pronghorn, have a disconcerting habit of running *toward* danger, rather than away from it. It would take a very brave coyote or family of coyotes to stand up to a charging herd of elk.

Hope Ryden, a wildlife writer investigating coyotes in Yellowstone National Park, was able to take pictures of a single young elk calf that successfully kept several coyotes away from the carcass of his dead friend, another elk of about the same age. When a coyote would sneak in for a nibble, the elk would charge, sending all the canines running helter-skelter. The calf kept the coyotes at bay for three days before finally wandering off.

Coyotes undoubtedly have had the contents of their stomachs and droppings examined more than any other animal on earth to see what they eat. Unfortunately the coyote must be dead before his stomach can be examined, but during years of local, state, and federal government trapping and poisoning there have been plenty of bellies to peer into. Thousands upon thousands, in fact. The studies have proven conclusively that a coyote will eat whatever is around that will hold still long enough, but that the largest proportion of food consumed is rodents, rabbits, carrion and insects. It would seem obvious from the things that coyotes consider tasty entrees that they are as much scavengers as they are predators.

In their roles as predators, coyotes have been accused by some as being decimators of game herds as well as water fowl. By others they are blessed as being a necessary part of the balance of nature in that they weed out the diseased and weak from the herds and flocks, thus improving the species and preventing excess population of game animals. Still others offer proof that coyotes and predators in general have very little effect on the population of either game animals or, for that matter, of rodents and rabbits. This disagreement has led to what might be called the "Great Predation Controversy" among wildlife biologists and naturalists.

The oldest of the theories upholds the idea of a balance in nature. It, in turn, supplanted the previous, mindless contention that all predators were vicious, worthless beasts which must be exterminated because they interfere with the interests of humans. That is, they eat livestock and remove game from the sights of hunters' guns.

The new theory that is gaining acceptance is that predation has no significant effect on game or rodent populations because the animals preyed upon would succumb to other natural causes even if there were no predators at all. It would follow, then, that if one species of predator were removed entirely from an ecosystem there would be little effect on species of prey. If coyotes, for instance, were removed, nature would fill the void with other predators such as bobcats and foxes. In other words, their populations could increase since competition from coyotes would have ceased.

The theory provides a handy rationale for exterminating coyotes. In South Dakota the theory was borne out. The coyote population was very effectively reduced and soon red foxes filled the void. Not part of the theory was the ranchers' response to too many foxes—get rid of them, too! If such a program of eliminating the predators that took the place of those previously removed were continued, we might be lucky to have a single mouse left to call wildlife.

In other areas, however, intensive efforts have been made to eliminate coyotes with poisons, cyanide guns, traps, bullets, and aircraft. And sure enough, nature replaced the dead coyotes with other predators—more coyotes than ever before! This diabolical coyote reaction to the purging of their kind from an ecosystem will be discussed in a later chapter.

The question remains, are coyotes gluttons when it comes to game animals and birds? Does their consumption of rodents help balance rodent populations? Or do they eat just the right amount to maintain a balance in nature? Or does it matter what they eat?

Aldo Leopold, one of the country's leading naturalists and a progenitor of the idea that led to our Wilderness System, said in 1947, "No recognized deer specialist has reported a case of effective deer control by coyotes." But in a Texas wildlife refuge study made during a six-year period there was no hunting of deer and no attempt to control predators. It was, in other words, a primitively natural situation. The biologists making the study found that the deer herd was stabilized by coyotes. The writer of the report, a recognized deer specialist and a biologist for the U. S. Bureau of Sport Fisheries and Wildlife, concluded his report by stating, "I personally feel that predators can exert significant effects upon the population levels of large game animals."

Paul Errington, a noted Iowa scientist, had concluded from studies of predation on various prey species by various predators (not including coyotes) that if predators do not remove excess prey, then some other factor will. He felt that habitat conditions, not predators, determine the size of population for a species.

But then a study made in Georgia revealed that the only likely effective control of the annual cycle of rodents would be by various species of predators getting to the scene in time to do something about excess populations.

And in an area in Germany where *all* the predators were exterminated by some deadly process, the rodents did not take over the world, but their population cycles began to fluctuate wildly. Great increases in populations were followed by massive deaths due to starvation, followed again by huge repopulations and so on in a vicious circle. This would seem to offer proof that the predators had maintained the delicate balance.

As you can see, the life sciences are not exact sciences, and biologists do not agree on much of anything concerning predation. One has to be wary of theories presented as facts by life scientists. Animal behavior observed in one particular ecosystem does not necessarily establish normal behavior for an entire species. More to the fact, animal behavior, habitat, weather, disease, parasites, relationships between predator and predator as well as between predator and prey, and innumerable other factors offer obscure sets of circumstances in seemingly endless sets of combinations that humans are simply not yet knowledgeable enough to understand fully.

Adding to the confusion is the fact that coyotes are

easily the most complex, certainly among the most adaptable, and quite possibly the most intelligent animals on the continent. Besides humans, of course.

Doomed by the Mayan god Hunabku to be forever hungry, the coyote continues to search for food, somehow overcoming all the obstacles humans put in his way. Perhaps the white man does not know of the power of the Navaho, bestowed on Coyote 'way back in the beginning of the Fifth World, which is the world we live in today.

When the Holy People were shaping the earth, say the Navaho, Coyote was often an unwelcome visitor to the great hogan in which the Holy People met. The first thing Coyote did when he barged in uninvited and unannounced was to run around and clean up all the scraps left over from the last meal. If any Holy Person was still eating, Coyote took that too.

Coyote always managed to know when the Holy People were going to plan something of interest to him. It was at such times that he interrupted them, often saving them from making terrible mistakes. Through his instructions they caused the plants to grow and bloom over the face of the barren earth. Because of his wisdom they gave him control over the vegetation, darkness and daylight, thunder and rain, lightning and all rainbows—in other words, power over the elements and the production of food, his favorite thing on earth.

5 · Coyote Society

During the night a little cool air had spilled down off the mountain peaks and settled in the bottom of Deep Canyon, a tiny part of the great Sonora Desert. For a few hours, before the searing desert sun rising over the canyon walls drove them to seek protection from the heat, the residents would flit and scurry about the parched, sandy stream bed searching for food.

At precisely thirty minutes past dawn, a roadrunner passed an indigo bush growing between two boulders. He stopped for a moment, raised his bristly topknot, and made a strange rattling sound in his throat. Every morning at the same time he passed the bush while on his rounds looking for a fat lizard or grasshopper. This morning he left his established trail, flipped over a few stones with his beak to see if breakfast could be beneath them, and hurried on his way, running as usual since he cannot fly.

High up in the branches of a smoke tree, a LeConte thrasher whistled at the dawn. On a rocky slope above the stream bed, a butcher-bird found a grasshopper and impaled it on the thorns of a jumping cholla cactus to be kept in storage for a later meal. Right now it was more important that he perch in the smoke tree and sing his warning to the canyon, "My territory! No other butcher-birds allowed!"

Beneath the tree a scorpion darted out from beneath a rock, scurried about with his poison tail arched at the ready over his back, then disappeared under another rock. A crested lizard scurried from a crack in a boulder and, as though belatedly terrified by the passing roadrunner, stood up on his hind legs and sped out of sight beneath a mesquite bush. A Merriam's kangaroo rat suddenly appeared beneath the smoke tree, then, just as suddenly, pounded his hind feet against the ground and bounced like his Australian namesake up the slope and out of sight. An antelope ground squirrel, his little tail curled over his back, hurried from his burrow and investigated boulder after boulder in his nervous way. Then, hearing an alien sound, he stood up on his hind legs and squeaked an alarm to all ground squirrels.

In the stream bed, just below a rock outcropping that was the site of a raging waterfall when a rare chubasco storm brought torrential rain to the arid desert, an animal was digging in the soft sand. He sent it flying in all directions for a time, then sat back on his haunches to pant and survey the hole, now three feet deep. This was Itsa, father-coyote, searching for the elusive, life-sustaining substance so seldom come by in his hot, dry environment.

He was digging for water and three feet was not enough. The bottom of the crater was as dry as the surface. Back into the hole he went, piling up a mound of sand under his belly with his front paws and kicking it out with his back paws.

Finally a stain appeared at the bottom of the hole. This seemed to give Itsa new energy and he dug more furiously than ever. Now wet, sandy globs were hurled up over the stream banks and Itsa did not pause to rest until a little pool of water seeped into the hole. Then he sat back, panting, waiting for the pool to get larger so he could have a well-earned drink.

It is in this manner that coyotes supply water for themselves and incidentally for all the other animals of the desert that need it. Some, like the Merriam's kangaroo rat, do not need it. They never drink water, their bodies long since having evolved so that they are able to extract sufficient moisture from their food.

The pool would serve Itsa in other ways too. Only birds and insects would drink from it during the day, but at dusk and through the night little mammals like the desert pack rat would come, and an alert coyote would have no trouble keeping his belly full. Later on, fairy shrimp and tadpoles might appear in the pool, which a quick coyote could snap out of the water for between-meal snacks.

Itsa drank his fill and trotted busily up out of the stream bed and onto the rocky slopes. There was much for a coyote to do before the desert heat became overpowering. He had a family to feed. His mate could not yet leave the

four still blind pups. He ran here and there among the boulders, clambering over them almost as agilely as a mountain goat, something his cousin coyotes of the prairies would not be able to do. He would have to wait until nightfall for his favorite food, the pack rat. There would be no digging that little rodent out of his nest, for he made it with jumping cholla and packed the entrance with the merciless cactus.

But perhaps he could find an antelope ground squirrel, the funny little striped rodent with an unusually short tail and ears so small it looks as though it has none at all. As Itsa bounced from rock to rock looking for one of these squirrels, which can withstand even the hottest sunlight, a bighorn ram, standing high on a ridge overlooking the canyon, turned his majestic head to watch the coyote's progress. The bighorn sheep, too, would be thankful for Itsa's water well.

Halfway up the side of the canyon an enormous boulder sheltered a shallow cave. Directly in front of the cave was a catclaw bush, a desert acacia covered with vicious, curved thorns that served well as an entrance guard. From behind the bush came the sounds of soft whines and an occasional tiny growl as Itowa nursed the little balls of fur that were her pups and waited for Itsa to return with breakfast.

When the pups were just a little older, she too would be able to go out into the cool morning to hunt. Soon she would nurse only in the mornings and evenings and leave the den at night. When the pups were about a month old and able to take solid food, both she and Itsa would leave to eat their fill. When they returned to the den, the pups would paw and lick their parents' muzzle—their way of asking to be fed. Then Itsa and Itowa would regurgitate food into the pups' mouths. Later still, the parents would take turns bringing back entire animals for the pups to devour. Until then the little fellows would take their food secondhand.

Not many fathers in the canine world help feed their young or help with the rearing in any way. The coyote and the wolf are exceptions. If a mother coyote is killed, the father will continue to raise the pups. Even if they are still nursing, the father will often try to feed them by regurgitating into their mouths. It is not necessary that the food be partially digested. The process is important as a way of carrying the food and as a method of reducing it to baby-food size.

61

When Itsa arrived at the den with his ground squirrel, he scrambled under the catclaw and laid the morsel in front of the cave. Itowa growled menacingly. Although she must have appreciated the meal, father coyotes are simply not welcome near the pups until they are about two or three weeks old, when they start tumbling about outside the cave. So Itsa wriggled out from under the catclaw, trotted to his favorite mesquite, and flopped down under it.

Itsa, of course, was a desert coyote, smaller than his prairie, mountain, or southwestern cousins. An average desert coyote weighs only twenty pounds as compared to a mountain coyote's sixty pounds and a prairie coyote's thirty pounds. One coyote trapped in Kansas weighed seventy-five pounds, the weight of a healthy wolf.

But Itsa was small due to the rigors of his arid climate and now, in the spring of the year, he looked even smaller since he was shedding his reddish gray fur. Unlike dogs, coyotes shed great strips and chunks of fur, the soft inner coat first and the outer coat last. Often strips of fur will trail on the ground until they are caught in brush and torn off. Coyotes will often rub against brush or rocks to hasten the shedding process. Bare skin appears in patches over the animal's body until he soon looks as if he were suffering from some terrible disease.

In the desert and other warm climates coyotes get the "summer mange," as the shedding has been called, in the spring. Prairie coyotes shed during the summer months, while mountain and northern coyotes do not shed until fall. With the latter, the change is not so drastic and they will have a new coat for winter in no time at all.

As Itsa napped under his mesquite bush and Itowa

finished her meal and rearranged the pups in the cave, the searing sunlight began to penetrate into the canyon depths. The din of animal sounds began to subside. The Merriam kangaroo rats buried themselves in the sand and the larger desert kangaroo rats scurried to their cool burrows. A kit fox hurried along the bighorn sheep trail toward its den.

A cacomixtle (ka-ko-mish'-tlay), the ring-tailed cat, cousin of the raccoon and coatimundi, peered down through the twigs of the smoke tree with his enormous round eyes. His bushy black-and-white ringed tail, as long as his body, hung down from the branches. A grasshopper mouse, late to retire for the day, threw back his tiny head like a wolf and squeaked a long shrill note. As if the sound reminded the cacomixtle that it was time for bed, he clambered down the tree and disappeared among the boulders. The butcher-bird ceased his warnings. Even the locusts stopped their harsh screechings.

Soon only the antelope ground squirrels could be seen, still dashing about the rocks in their incessant search for food. The boulder-strewn slopes shimmered in the scorching heat. Not the slightest breeze stirred the air. All but the squirrels drowsed.

Suddenly Itsa raised his head. The hair of his mane began to rise and a low growl rattled in his throat. In an area undisturbed by humans, a coyote knows his territory well. He knows the smells and sounds of all the animals, whether his prey, his enemies, or his competitors. Now a new odor struck his nostrils—the odor of his own species but a stranger. Another coyote had entered his territory!

Itsa slowly emerged from beneath the mesquite bush and sniffed the air, but he saw nothing unusual. Quickly he bounded up a series of rocks to the top of the boulder that sheltered his den. There below him on the bighorn trail trotted a large male coyote. He too sniffed the air as though he had caught the scent of Itsa.

Itsa leaped down from the boulder and stood in the trail to meet the intruder, his mane fully raised and his tail held straight out to show dominance. The stranger trotted around the boulder and stopped quickly at the menacing sight of Itsa, now grimacing with his mouth pulled tightly back. The stranger tensed his muscles a moment, but then he advanced slowly, lowering his hindquarters with his back slightly arched. As he crept toward Itsa he continually looked away, then back at Itsa, while flicking his tongue in and out in a licking motion. This was a sign of submission and friendliness, but Itsa would have none of it. As soon as the stranger reached him, Itsa charged forward, his muzzle wrinkled and his mouth gaping wide as if to bite. The intruder immediately rolled over onto his back. Itsa planted his front paws firmly on the stranger's chest, growling and snarling furiously.

There was no other way in which the trespassing coyote could express his submission, so he just cringed as if waiting for the slash at his throat. But that was not the coyote way and finally Itsa turned aside, although still bristling and growling. As soon as he was released, the stranger leaped to his feet and hurried back up the trail the way he had come. Itsa returned to his station under the mesquite and was soon asleep.

Had Itsa not been grumpy due to his "summer mange" and defensive because of his nearby mate and pups, the meeting with the stranger might have gone differently. Although coyotes are strongly territorial and not at all social animals like wolves and dogs, Itsa might have tolerated the intruder for a short visit. Then Itsa could have established his dominance simply by holding out his tail. The other coyote could have accepted his inferior status by displaying a "submissive grin," which is essentially the same grimace that Itsa used to threaten the stranger except that the teeth are *not* bared. That small difference is very important to coyotes. It could be important for humans to remember the difference too, because dogs use the same method to express threats or friendliness.

When all the grimacing and grinning was over, serious investigation would begin with sniffing each other. One of the more important sniffing areas for all canines is the supracaudal gland, which is located under the tail at its base under a dark patch of fur. The gland produces a faint odor which is presumably pleasant-smelling to canines. The odor is especially strong in coyotes.

After a thorough investigation the coyotes might then play awhile, although not long and hard as wolves and dogs might do. Coyotes are not noted for their tolerance, and any accidental hurt might lead to a furious battle. Dr. Michael Fox, in a study of several canine species in captivity, discovered that most of the animals liked to chase and frolic about, even with species not their own. But toward the end of the first year of age the coyotes become increasingly less tolerant of play, finally even snapping and snarling at much larger wolves who only wanted to romp. But even as puppies, coyotes became very angry if their playmates got too rough.

In the wilds, coyotes have been known to try to get dogs to play. One moonlit night many years ago on our ranch in the Laguna Mountains of southern California we went to the door to investigate the barking of our German Shepherd dog. A few feet in front of the dog a coyote was crouched down with her rump up in the air just as dogs do when they want to play. But when the Shepherd stopped barking and approached a little closer, the coyote would dart away only to come back and crouch down again. She continued to do this each time the dog approached, obviously wanting him to chase her. But our dog never got the idea and the coyote finally seemed to give up in disgust and trotted off. An old-timer in the area told us that coyotes often solicited play in order to lure an unsuspecting dog away from the house and behind a boulder or brush where "a pack of coyotes" would be waiting to pounce on the dog. We have not heard the theory before or since.

Coyotes do occasionally play or try to play with animals outside the dog family. At times coyotes and ravens seem to play a game. The raven will land tauntingly in front of the coyote, who will make a sudden dart for the bird. The raven will hop or glide a few feet away and the mock chase continues in that fashion. It cannot be assumed that the coyote is actually trying to catch the raven to eat it because shortly after the game they might very well be seen resting or feeding side by side.

That there can be a bond between coyotes and ravens, as well as other carrion-eating birds, has long been noted. Some authorities think that ravens are the most intelligent of all birds and others think that coyotes are the most intelligent of the dog family. So they make a good team as the bird shares in the coyote's kill and sets up a clamor to warn the canine of danger. When coyotes first appeared in the New England states not long ago it was reported that ravens came with them. Neither ravens nor coyotes had ever been seen in the Northeast before.

And coyotes seem to delight in pestering badgers, nipping them on the rump, crouching down in front of them, and running circles around the stodgy badgers when they are patiently trying to make progress in digging after a rodent or simply plodding home. It is usually reported that the badger tries his best to ignore the foolish coyote.

The Yokuts Indians of central California once said that Eagle Chief asked his people to build the Sierra Nevada Mountains so he would have a place to escape from Coyote's constant pestering.

When the pups were about three months old, Itsa and Itowa began to take them on nightly hunts. School had begun. First they would go to their well for a long drink. Of course the pups had to be snarled at to keep them from splashing in the water. It was too soon for the pups to be patient enough to wait quietly by the well to see what fat rodent would come to drink. So the family scoured the rocky slopes for food, and on rare occasions the pups were attentive enough actually to see their parents catch a rat or a mouse and thereby learn their lessons.

Itsa's family territory was about one square mile, and as the summer nights passed, the pups had soon investigated almost every bush and boulder. When the pups were full-grown they would establish their own territories. They would learn the location of every rabbit trail and the little pits along the trail where the rabbits dusted themselves to get rid of lice and fleas. They would learn where the pack rat nests were, and where the ground squirrel, mouse, and

kangaroo rat burrows were. When the little rodents were scarce, they would learn to find the bitter juniper berries on the slopes of the mountains near Deep Canyon. They would learn where to find the mesquite bushes to use for shade and for food when the screw bean pods were ripe. And if they were brave coyotes, they would learn that they could steal the sweet fruits of the date palms from the human world in the valley below the desert hills.

And they would learn the proper way for coyotes to travel in the hot, rocky landscape. As much as possible, they would course along the sandy arroyos in the skimpy shade of the paloverde trees. The thorny "green-trees" have no leaves most of the year but they grow densely along the washes and offer a little shelter from the sun. Too, the soft sand of arroyos is much easier on coyote feet.

The pups were taught many things to do and many things not to do. They learned the hard way, for example, not to try to dig the desert pack rat from his prickly nest. They learned the hard way that the bobcat, the spotted skunk, and the raccoon were not animals that coyotes attacked or played with. They somehow sensed that the massive curved horns and sharp hoofs of the bighorn ram would have to be reckoned with if they bothered a lamb. And they found that rodents and lizards were good, nutritious fare for coyotes, young and old.

Part of the night's work was in posting their area with "keep-out signs." They established scent posts by urinating on bushes or boulders or tree trunks or, lacking these, even on piles of their own feces to mark the boundaries of their territory. Most canids, including dogs, do this but with dogs it seems to have lost all meaning.

By late fall there were only two pups left. The others succumbed to any one of a hundred diseases and parasites that plague all wildlife. The surviving pups were ready to go out into the world. Itsa and Itowa were making it increasingly plain that it was expected of them. It seemed such a short time ago that Itsa had played with them when they tumbled about, nipping at his ears and tail, but now he growled at them often and Itowa had even snapped at them. When the family hunted together the parents no longer shared with the pups, and snarled furiously if they came near the kill.

So one evening one of the pups gave a long chase after a brush rabbit and never returned. Within a few weeks the other pup had disappeared in the same manner. That is the coyote way of making certain that their population will not exceed their food supply. Nature's way, through disease, is to reduce litters by about fifty percent. Where man leaves the coyote alone, the litters average four to five pups but where man poisons and traps, the litters can average five to seven or even more. In either case only about half survive.

In a study made in Texas, coyote pups old enough to disperse from the home territory were caught, tagged, and then released. The average distance traveled by female pups seeking new territories was over twenty-five miles. For males the average was ten and a half miles. However, many of the pups had traveled fifty miles and several had gone a full hundred. The distance young coyotes would have to travel would depend on the competition for territory. Texas has a lot of coyotes and unclaimed land is hard to come by. It is possible that Itsa's pups would only have to go a few miles before they could stake a claim in the desert.

The story of Itsa and his family assumes that humans had not disturbed the Deep Canyon ecosystem. There are few such places left. In these days it is almost impossible to study the ecology of the coyote without considering that poisons, traps, and bullets are part of the coyotes' environment. In fact, one theory contends that human attempts to reduce coyote populations have only succeeded in creating a kind of "super coyote" that relies more on predation than scavenging and is therefore more likely to prey on large game animals and livestock. Simultaneously, those animals which do rely on scavenging would be the first ones and perhaps the only ones to die from eating poisoned bait.

But leading authorities on wildlife, such as Dr. A. Starker Leopold of the University of California and Dr. E.

Raymond Hall of the University of Kansas, disagree. They say there is no evidence that there has been any basic genetic change in the species as a whole, but that individuals or even large numbers of coyotes do respond in various ways to the unnatural pressures imposed on them by attempts to control their population.

As an example, it was noticed that cyanide guns, otherwise known as "coyote-getters," had lost their effectiveness not too many years after they were introduced into the world of the coyote. Trappers found that coyotes had been urinating, defecating, and scratching dirt on the guns. The conclusion was that parent coyotes were teaching their pups to avoid them.

Coyotes, being uncommonly quick to learn, marked the lesson well when one of their numbers tugged at the bait on a coyote-getter and got a wad loaded with cyanide in his mouth from which he quickly died. It is also argued that if a coyote eats from a carcass baited with poison and survives after a sickness, he may well rely on predation rather than on carrion for his food from then on. It can be assumed that the sicker but wiser coyote might also teach his pups to avoid carrion and rely on prey, large and small.

But there is a much more dramatic and certain effect on coyote society when their numbers are unnaturally reduced by humans. Most of the higher animals except humans regulate their own population to suit their environment. That is, if they are becoming overcrowded, thus putting a strain on the food supply, they automatically mate less and have fewer babies.

This would happen, too, if the food supply should be reduced for any other reason, such a drought or a high death rate among the prey species. As an example, a survey made in the Curlew Valley of Utah showed that the coyotes there depend on the jackrabbit for seventy-five percent of their food. When the jackrabbit populations were reduced, the numbers of coyotes were also soon reduced.

If, on the other hand, there is a surplus of food, mating and littering will increase. The surplus might be due to better environmental conditions, to a high population peak of the prey animals, or to a large dent made in the coyote population. When large numbers of coyotes have been killed off from whatever cause, a kind of vacuum has been created. Sooner or later it is filled, not only with a greater number of young adults from the larger litters, but also with coyotes wandering in from other areas. All are seeking to establish their own territories, and the competition becomes fierce. Their society is completely disrupted and if any territories are established at all, they are reduced in size so that there are more coyotes per square mile than before.

This all puts quite a strain on the food supply as well as on the coyote temperament. Some will likely get desperate and prey on animals not previously included in their diets, such as sheep. It is possible that once the desperadoes become efficient at killing livestock they may continue to do so, long after populations become stable again when there is law and order among coyotes once more. It would seem that where humans deliver massive doses of poisons to coyotes they only create greater problems for themselves.

The coyote is known in scientific language as *Canis latrans*, which means "barking dog," although "singing dog" would have been a better name. He is one of the eight species of the genus *Canis*; the others being the gray wolf, the red wolf of the southern United States, the dingo of Australia, three species of jackals which live in Europe and Africa, and the plain old familiar dog, whose Latin name is *Canis familiaris*.

Of all these the coyote is probably more similar to the jackals, but in behavior more than in appearance. All the others of the genus are social animals, but the coyote and the jackals are not. Jackals, like coyotes, hunt singly or in pairs and are well known for their cunning. The side-striped jackal and the golden jackal are noted for their singing voices.

The four North American members of the genus have the same number of chromosomes and therefore could interbreed. They usually do not. But there are known cases of interbreeding among coyotes and dogs, causing some concern that a race of coy-dogs might be created. A male dog is sexually potent all year, so theoretically he could mate with a female coyote even though she is in heat only once a year as compared to the female dog's two periods of heat, or oestrus.

But coyotes go through three or four weeks of "courtship" before mating. The female has to select a prospective father with care, since he must help feed her and the pups after they are born. Male dogs do not help with the feeding at all, thus the chances of coy-dog pups surviving in the wilds are considerably lessened. And since dogs do not court before mating, it would be a rare occasion for a female coyote even to consider a dog. Even in captivity under controlled conditions it was found to be very difficult to get coyotes to breed with dogs.

A male coyote is sexually potent only four months of the

73

year and this, of course, coincides with the oestrus period of the female coyotes. The two oestrus cycles of dogs are earlier and later than that of coyotes but it is possible that a mateless male coyote could breed with a female dog if the cycles overlapped. It would be unusual. As a final blow to the idea of a race of hybrids, coy-dogs that have been studied showed breeding cycles of once a year, but three to four months before the heat period of coyotes.

Argument still continues as to whether the red wolf is really a true wolf or a cross between a coyote and gray wolf. The best evidence indicates that it is a true wolf. But it is a rapidly vanishing species, mostly due to persecution by humans and changing of the environment. Also, so few in number are the red wolves that it is certain that they are now cross-breeding with coyotes. One way or another, there will soon be no more red wolves.

It is not likely that gray wolves and coyotes interbreed very often. Wolves are normally very intolerant of their little cousins in the wilds. But there is one story that tells of a bond between wolves and coyotes. Back in the 1930's when the massive and successful attempt to exterminate wolves was drawing to a close, there were a few scattered lone wolves left. These loners almost invariably became killers, whether out of revenge against humans or out of the desperation of their loneliness no one will ever know. They destroyed entire flocks of sheep and large numbers of cattle in single attacks, often without eating any of their victims. Most of them managed to elude the traps and poisons of the government's finest trappers for many years.

Each of these renegade wolves was given a name by the distraught ranchers, partly out of fear and hatred and partly out of respect. One of the wolves, considered by

74

some the most destructive of all and thought by many to be a ghost, was called the Custer wolf. He was white and not very large but he was very wise. He was not often seen but he left his calling card of death somewhere in South Dakota quite often.

When he was seen, mostly in the distance, there were always two coyotes with him. They were his outriders and they ran slightly ahead of the wolf, one on either side, almost as if they were guiding him. At night when ranchers heard a lonely wolf-howl, two coyote voices always answered.

Finally, one day, the government trapper who had been trailing the wolf for months saw the trio and managed to shoot the coyotes. Not long afterward, the wolf became uncharacteristically very careless. Almost as though on purpose, he got caught in the kind of trap setup he had evaded for years. Even then he tore the trap from its anchor and dragged it for miles before the trapper caught up to end the Custer wolf's life.

The Paiute Indians often spoke of coyotes and wolves as brothers, with Coyote as the younger and the smaller of the two. In most of the tales the mischievous and disobedient Coyote continually taxes brother Wolf's patience. At one time, except for size, the brothers looked alike until one day Coyote went too far, as this story indicates.

One day Itsa, the Coyote, saw many people coming who were armed for war and ran to tell his brother, Isha. Isha armed himself and told Itsa to stay in the wickiup and not to look out or he, Isha, would surely be killed. Wolf went outside and soon Itsa heard the sounds of battle.

The fighting raged for many hours and finally Itsa could restrain his curiosity no longer. He looked outside, and as soon as he did Isha fell dead with an arrow in his heart. Itsa was so overcome with shame and remorse that he tried to burn himself to death but, of course, Coyote cannot die.

After the people left with Wolf's scalp as a war trophy, Itsa went out and ate his brother up, bones and all. Then, disguising himself, he went to the enemy camp and stole his brother's scalp. This he buried in the ground and watered the spot for six days. On the seventh day he heard his brother call and there was Isha, who was very angry.

"Who ate my flesh and bones?" asked Isha, and Itsa said he had not.

76

"Who ate my heart and liver?" asked Isha, and Itsa said he had not.

But finally Itsa admitted his crime and Isha said he must be taught a lesson. Wolf took a stick and hit his brother on the head so many times that his ears grew long and his nose became small. Then Wolf pulled on Itsa's teeth and made them long and ugly. This made Itsa very sad so that he cried, for he had been very proud of his pretty teeth.

And that is the way Coyote is today, with his long ears and little nose pointed at the moon, wailing over the loss of his pretty teeth.

6 · Our Good Friend Coyote

In the early days of the Fifth World, the Holy People, having sanctified the four sacred mountains which support the sky, knew it was time to sow the barren earth with seed. From the Lower World they brought up the Dew of Dawn, the Dew of Evening Twilight, the Dew of the Blue Sky, and the Dew of Darkness. They mixed them together and there came into existence Male Rain and Female Rain to make vegetation possible.

Then the Holy People talked of how plants should grow. They talked of many ways and decided that plants should grow in neat rows in special places.

But Coyote said, "You have no sense at all! Things must

be on earth with no special order anywhere on its surface." He told them that if plants grew in rows in special places, they could easily be destroyed by enemies. But that if they were placed at random throughout the earth they would be safe and would grow again and again.

So they set the sun and the moon in position and scattered the seeds of the plants at random about the earth. Then they told Talking God to sanctify them—to give them life. But Coyote said that he wanted to be the one to sanctify them. The Holy People were horrified. Imagine Coyote as the sanctifier of growing things! Coyote said, "All right, go ahead without me. See what happens."

Talking God began to tremble-run to do the sanctifying. But the sun and the moon did not move and the plants did not grow. It was the first time Talking God had failed. "Coyote's mind is behind this," someone said. "All right, Old Man," said First Man to Coyote, "you do it. You do it and a name will be made for you. And with things that are going to be made on this earth, your plans will never be ignored."

"Now that's the way people should talk to a person," said Coyote and he tremble-ran toward the sun and moon, toward the Grand Corn and all the other plants from the east. He tremble-ran toward them from the north, from the west, and from the south. And they were sanctified. The sun and the moon raised up and the plants grew to a great height.

The Navaho Indians, who tell many such legends of Coyote and the Holy People, had Coyote to thank for "fixing up the most important things of living to be." The Holy People prepared the earth for the human beings yet to come, and they were often on the verge of making disastrous errors until Coyote set them thinking in the right way. They usually accepted his advice grudgingly.

In the tales of many of the western tribes Coyote was responsible for many of the blessings bestowed on man. When they lived in eternal darkness, he brought them the sun. When they had no way to cook their food or keep themselves warm, he brought them fire. In the days when no one died and the earth was becoming overcrowded, he brought them death. He taught the Indians how to obtain their food and how to dance and how to sing.

In the Northwest, he often saved whole tribes from being devoured by monsters who lived in the great rivers like the Columbia in Washington or the Clearwater in Idaho. For the benefit of the Patwin of Central California, he even created rattlesnakes and ordered them to crawl along the ground and kill all the evil people. All the Patwin knew that rattlesnakes never bite good people.

The Mandans, who once lived in North Dakota, complained that their dogs, having the power of speech, were always tattling on their masters' wives and causing trouble. Coyote made it so that dogs could only bark. When the Mandans complained that the elk were eating too many people, Coyote changed the animals' nature so that they only ate grass. And he dimmed the eyesight of the bison so they would be easier for the Indian to hunt.

And so, even though mischievous and sometimes evil and often ludicrous, Coyote was the Indians' good friend.

But the white man asks, "Well, what good are coyotes, anyway?" A fair answer might be another question, "What good are you?" In environmental terms a human being may find it difficult to claim any more importance than a coyote.

People have a need, it seems, to evaluate the existence of all living things in terms of their own benefit. There is a word that defines this arrogance and it is "anthropocentric," meaning the universe considered as centered around human beings. But there has been a growing tendency of late to consider the worth of an animal species in some other light than the human profit-and-loss statement. These new values ascribed to the coyote are still anthropocentric, as we shall see, but they are a vast improvement as far as the coyote is concerned.

In the past twenty years or so, millions of city people have discovered the wilderness—not just the national parks and wilderness areas, but the forests and deserts and mountains and vast tracts of land administered by the federal Bureau of Land Management—and they have discovered the nation's wildlife. It has been obvious to these people that coyotes and other predators are a natural part of those lands and are therefore part of their natural heritage.

The worth of the coyote to these people might simply be the chance to see one or to hear its song in the wilderness night. Others might appreciate the beauty of his form and the grace of his movement, or marvel at the brightness of his tawny eyes. These are esthetic values, invaluable to the human spirit.

Since the advent of public awareness of our wildlife heritage it has often been said of coyotes that they belong not to just those few who seem convinced they would benefit by the animal's destruction, but to all the people of the United States. An even more enlightened view was expressed as the theme of the American pavilion at the recent World's Fair in Spokane, Washington: "The earth

81

does not belong to man, man belongs to the earth." It goes without saying that by "earth" is meant the soil and all the natural things in it and on it. It is a theme that was fully understood long ago by every American Indian clan, tribe, and nation. Coyotes, then, belong to the ecosystem—the community of living things—of which we are but a part.

An Advisory Committee on Predator Control submitted a lengthy report to the Secretary of the Interior in 1971. The document is called the "Cain Report" after the former Assistant Secretary of the Interior Stanley Cain, who was the chairman of the committee. The report called for a re-evaluation and lessening of predator control but stated, "We suspect the ecosystem would function without the coyote, but would be in some sense poorer." It might be added that we would be poorer to lose a wildlife heritage that is found nowhere else but on our continent. But for that matter, think of how well the ecosystem would function without us.

The Research Director of the Massachusetts Audubon Society, certainly a friend of animals, has said, "the major value of the large predators is the human value." By that he means that the large predators serve no purpose in the ecosystem and that their only value lies in what man ascribes to them. In other words, either God or nature made a mistake in creating animals that are useless. But if the statement is true, the coyote is indeed in danger. Human values are too often secondary to economic values.

The only statement that can be made about the value of the coyote is that we do not know nearly enough about the complex relationship between living things to say how much of an effect the disappearance of any one of them would have on the environment. Consider the audacity of proclaiming an entire species to be unessential, having only incidental value for humans, when we know relatively little about the species itself and not much more about the ecosystem in which it lives.

The scientific "facts" about the coyote are hard to come by. His food habits have been studied in various areas and numerous trappers have reported on the "personality" traits of individual coyotes. There have been limited studies by wildlife biologists, most of whom were employed by agencies dedicated to the "management" of wildlife. When the practice of "management" is extended to coyotes, it means killing them. But no significant, serious study has been made by a naturalist or ethologist, a scientist who studies animal behavior. Such studies seem to be reserved for species that are rare or endangered. Until such studies are made we will continue to know little about the coyote. And, of course, to be valid the studies must be made in the animal's natural habitat, not in the laboratory.

Even if it were true that the removal of coyotes would have no effect on the environment, they do now exist in it and do have an effect on it. If one coyote takes a fawn out of an overpopulated herd, eats a dead cow on the range, removes a diseased pronghorn antelope from the prairie, or catches a jackrabbit on an overgrazed pasture, he is in fact benefiting the environment. Perhaps the basic argument is really whether the animal is a greater benefit to the environment than it is a detriment to the sheep industry.

The value of the coyote becomes evident from records from around the country. A study made in Kansas concluded that the benefits from coyote predation on rodents and rabbits exceeded the losses from predation on livestock and poultry. It was estimated that in an average year each coyote living on or near a farm saved the farmer twenty-one dollars' worth of grass or crops by eating the rabbits and mice that would otherwise have eaten the grass or crops. Even considering the average loss of livestock to coyotes, the farmer still came out ahead.

On an Experimental Range Station in the Sierra Nevada foothills it was reported that coyotes "grazing" in the pastures with beef cattle subsisted almost solely on the rabbits and rodents that were competing with the ranchers' cattle for grass.

In a report from the Curlew Valley in Utah and Idaho was the information that three fourths of coyote diet on the range land was jackrabbit. Even back in 1875 George Bird Grinnell reported that "where all coyotes and wolves have been killed or driven off, the hares exist in great numbers but where the former are abundant, the latter are seldom seen."

In the Southwest recently there was a rather successful drive to exterminate the coyotes from an area with the intention of increasing the numbers of quail. With the coyotes gone, the losses of quail soared even higher. A short study revealed why. The major food of the coyotes was the cotton rats. The major food of the cotton rats was quail. Coyotes were immediately put on the protected list. People finally had discovered that the coyote was their good friend.

An incidental benefit, and perhaps also a study in courage or desperation, is the coyotes' penchant for porcupine. The prickly little rodent can cause considerable damage in forests since he lives on new buds, leaves and, worst of all, the bark of trees. Once he gnaws a ring of bark off a tree, it will die. When one considers that a porcupine with its barbed quills can weigh as much as or more than a coyote, it can be seen what great skill it takes to make a meal of it.

A single coyote will worry the porcupine, making sure to keep away from its tail with which he drives the quills into his attacker's face. A patient coyote will finally get his chance, since the rodent is slow and not very cautious and,

with a lightning flash of his paw under the porcupine's chin, flip him over. Once the soft belly is exposed, the coyote may prepare for dinner.

Two coyotes working together have an easier time. One worries the rodent from behind while the other waits for his chance with a right to the jaw. However, many coyotes have been trapped or killed with their muzzles full of quills, indicating that they needed a little more practice.

Of course, the primary natural function of the coyote is to exist. There are many who think he has that right. But humans like to think of animals in terms of their value as functional units. So, among the natural functions of the coyote that give it value to the environment and therefore to humans are its feeding habits. It serves as a carrion eater and as a predator of weak and diseased hoofed animals of the wilds.

The Cain Report, reflecting the opinion of a number of scientists, stated that there are so many vertebrate and invertebrate scavengers that the coyote's role as a carrion eater must be minor. But aside from the bear, which sometimes eats carrion, the coyote is the largest scavenger left in the United States in any significant numbers now that the wolf is virtually gone. It would seem that the speed with which a group of coyotes could dispose of a carcass would make them our most important scavenger as compared to insects, smaller mammals, and birds, including even the vulture.

Adolph Murie, a naturalist once employed by the U.S. Fish and Wildlife Service at Yellowstone National Park, at one time watched for several hours as numerous coyotes came and went almost in procession to the carcass of an elk. After the skeleton was cleaned, a new crew started on the bones.

Murie wrote of an encounter with an outraged resident of Yellowstone National Park who reported that he had seen coyotes devouring a deer. When Murie investigated he found over a hundred botfly larvae, each over an inch long, packed into the deer's nasal passages and sinuses. There was no fat on the animal, indicating that if a coyote had killed the deer, it had performed a service to the environment. It had eliminated from the herd a weakened carrier of parasites that would have died from suffocation or starvation anyway.

Whether or not coyotes are a significant factor in controlling deer population, they certainly help. And any help at all is exceedingly important when a deer herd gets too large. There is nothing more destructive to forest or range land than overgrazing and overbrowsing.

A few people have discovered still another value in the coyote—as a pet. Certain problems are reported, however. A coyote is much more active and inquisitive than a dog. He is curious about what is under almost anything and he seems to feel that anything soft should have a hole dug in it. This includes mattresses, sofas, and armchairs. And, of course, a hole must be dug in the rug to see what is under it. Coyotes also love leather for the oil in it. A closetful of shoes would provide dessert for a week.

One of the delights that go with a house coyote is that he will sing at the drop of a musical note. Many photographs have appeared in books and magazines that feature animals, showing a family group sitting on the sofa or lounging on the floor with a coyote, all with their heads thrown back in a community sing.

Many people have become disillusioned with their pet coyotes, usually because they expected them to act like dogs. But an essentially wild animal, no matter how much of a pet, cannot be expected to act like an animal that has been domesticated for thousands of years. Do anything to a coyote that he could take to be aggressive or hostile and he is very likely to defend himself no matter how well he knows the person. The threat of a bath, for instance, could be mistaken by a coyote to be a very hostile act.

On the other hand, a few years ago in suburban San Diego a lady noticed a stray dog playing with her own dog in the front yard. Having a soft spot in her heart for strays, she decided to adopt it since it got along so well with her dog. But first it had to have a bath, as it was filthy. After a bit of a struggle she caught the stray, lugged it into the garage, and plopped it into a tub of water. It meekly and mournfully submitted to a thorough scrubbing.

Wondering what breed of dog it might be, she asked a number of friends and neighbors if they knew. Several days later a friend identified it positively. It was a coyote.

A young woman in Wyoming raised fifteen coyotes in large enclosures. She found that although she was, in effect, their mother, having bottle-fed them as pups, doctored cuts and scratches, even washed their faces with a warm cloth to simulate a mother's tongue, only one became really tame. And even that one, when given a choice between freedom and the soft life of a pet, chose the wilds. The others were politely friendly but always cautious and sometimes surly.

Perhaps coyotes resent confinement, even when raised without ever having known freedom. It seems that coyotes that have been befriended by humans but allowed to remain free develop a closer attachment to the humans.

A family in northern California, however, have a pet coyote who is very affectionate between his periods of utter mischief. He may chew a bar of soap until he foams at the mouth, tear a pillow apart to see the feathers fly, convert a fine leather hassock into his toy box by pulling all the stuffing out, empty the salt shakers all over the floor, attack a hot-water bottle under the bedclothes with very wet results, ruin the living room curtains while chasing a moth, and dig a tunnel under the cement garden walk, but he does jump up into his master's arms for licks and kisses and that makes up for the rest. But he has the run of the house and yard and is no more confined than the humans are when they are home.

Some fortunate people have befriended coyotes in the wild, an experience that in many ways must be more satisfying than having a pet coyote. In such cases the animals can be enjoyed in their natural environment and their normal behavior observed.

Many years ago Lila Lofberg in her book *Sierra Outpost* told of how she and her husband had accepted a lonely job as dam tenders in the high country of the Sierra Nevada Mountains. They were snowbound and alone throughout most of the winter. The only way in or out at the time was on snowshoes, a dangerous journey under the best conditions. One particularly severe winter just at dusk during a fierce storm the couple saw an almost completely starved coyote not twenty feet from their kitchen door.

When the man opened the door to toss out some food, the coyote did not budge. She was belly-deep in the snow and could not have moved far or fast in any event. The man closed the door and he and his wife watched from the kitchen window as the coyote inched toward the food.

The following day the coyote was found sitting on a rise in the snow a short distance from the house. When food was tossed in her direction she retrieved it, trotted back to her resting place, and laid it in the snow without eating it, then watched the humans to see what would happen next. When more food was tossed she repeated the process. But she ate nothing until the humans went back into the house. Then she nibbled leisurely at her dinner as though she had been eating regularly all along.

The people fed the coyote morning and night for three days, and on the fourth morning a second coyote sat waiting for breakfast. He too followed the pattern of trotting to get the food where it landed in the snow, then taking it back to the rise in the snow to drop it and wait. It was obvious at once that they were mates. The Lofbergs called them Tom and Jerry. The coyotes learned their names immediately, so that when the man threw out food and called "Jerry," only she came forward. It was the same with Tom.

On the morning of the seventh day after Jerry had practically knocked at the door, a third coyote was waiting for breakfast. But he was more cautious than the other two had been and had to be coaxed by Jerry to approach the food. This she did by trotting back and forth between the food and the newcomer, finally sticking her nose in the food and letting the cautious one smell her nose.

The late arrival was named Dick. Once over his fear, he did not obey the rules set by the other coyotes but snapped up the food no matter which name was called. But one day the woman screamed at him in exasperation, and from that time on Dick took his proper turn when called, carrying the food back to his resting place and waiting politely as did the others. However, he varied the routine just a bit. When the food was tossed for him he stood up on his hind legs and hopped over to pick it up. He continued to do his little dance every time he was fed during the two years the couple knew him.

The Lofbergs got to know several more coyotes during the remaining three years of their stay in the mountains. They lost some of their friends to traps and to those who can think of nothing better to do in the wilds but to kill wild things. Other coyotes came to take their places but with different personalities, lacking the charm of Dick, the clown coyote who danced for his food. By the time the couple left to take another job, only Tom was there to see them go.

Those coyotes and their human friends had become quite close but the animals remained wild, visiting the Lofbergs frequently in the summer months for a snack and virtually depending on them for food in the winter when the snow was deep and loose, making hunting impossible.

Much more recently in the hills near San Diego, California, the purchaser of a little plot of land in the chaparral brush country immediately discovered that a coyote was a resident before him. Instead of running for his shotgun and clearing his land of "varmints," he set out varied amounts of food and water and ran for his camera. With a little time and patience he found there was a family of coyote residents. Eventually he could approach some of them to take a few pictures and chat awhile.

When he planted a garden he sowed enough seed so there would be sufficient strawberries and tomatoes to satisfy the famous coyote "fruit tooth." Some of the family would disappear for several months at a time, but just when he would come to suspect the worst they would reappear one day at the water bucket or in the strawberry patch. Others, of course, he never saw again.

All in all it would seem that the benefits of coyotes to the environment and to humans far outweigh the disadvantages. In the main he has served humanity well ever since the time, eons ago, after the earth had been shaped and vegetated by Coyote and the Holy People and an anger divided them from one another. The anger became so intense that First Man and First Woman fled to the end of the earth. Coyote chose to follow them and has been our good friend ever since. Someday, perhaps, humans will have the wisdom to realize it.

7 · Coyote's Worst Enemy

"The animal of this country called Coyotl is very sagacious in waylaying. When he wishes to attack, he firsts casts his breath over the victim to stupefy it. Diabolical indeed is the creature."

That was the first recorded European impression of the *coyotl*, the Aztec name from which we derived the name coyote. It was written about 1560 by the friar Bernardino de Sahagun in a book concerning New Spain, now called Mexico. Since that time the attitude of whites toward the coyote has gotten steadily worse and not much more accurate.

The history of the whites' relationship with the coyote,

and most other predators, is neither intelligent nor pleasant. Prejudice against the coyote got off to an early start during the frontier days. Settlers complained of attacks by predators on their livestock. As settlement increased, so did complaints and demands for war against the "vicious beasts of prey." A folklore began to develop about the animals which made them into cunning superkillers whose only desire in life was to ravage everything within sight and smell, just for fun.

A senator from Wyoming, who also just happened to be a sheepman, spoke angrily of the well-meaning people who just did not understand about the ". . . terrific disaster wrought upon herds and flocks by wolves and coyotes or with the method employed by these animals in connection with the destruction of their prey. It is the most barbarous thing imaginable."

Magazine writers accepted the wildly imaginative figures of the ranchers and wrote of "thousands of sheep, calves and colts being killed by coyotes alone each year." People in the West began to fear attacks from marauding bands of coyotes in spite of the well-known fact that coyotes do not run in packs.

It was almost a very successful war. Cougars, once plentiful throughout the country, are now a rare species. The gray wolf is now an endangered species in the contiguous United States and is found only in Michigan, Minnesota, and Wisconsin in small numbers. The California grizzly and many other subspecies have long been extinct and there are only an estimated 850 grizzlies left in the Rockies. Countless thousands of martens, fishers, wolverines, skunks, otters, and other fur-bearing animals were exterminated. As usual, the natural consequences

Shaded area shows original range of the red wolf (*Canis rufus*), now found only on the Gulf coast of Texas and Louisiana.

Shaded area shows original range of the gray wolf (*Canis lupus*), now relegated to the Lake Superior region of Michigan and northern border of Minnesota. Individuals have been reported in Idaho, Montana, and Wyoming.

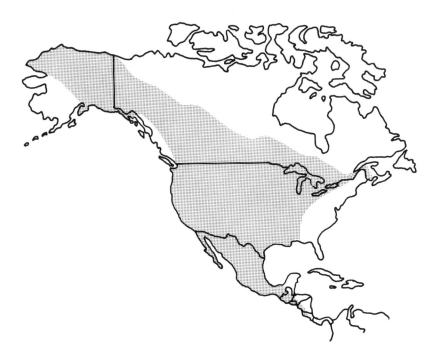

Shaded area of map shows present range of the coyote (*Canis latrans*). No one really knows original range.

had not been anticipated. Coyotes expanded their range unbelievably as though they thrived on poison and traps.

Meantime, the public began to have a love affair with the grazing animals which, like deer and elk, it had previously been killing off at a tremendous rate. Somehow it became sinful and savage for predators to kill grazing animals for their food. Hostility against the wolf, the cougar, the coyote, and even the bear grew to preposterous proportions.

Then the war of extermination began. Federal, territorial, state, and local governments moved their arsenals against the predators. Bounties were paid. Poisoning and trapping were done on a massive scale. The officials were joined in the campaign by ranchers, hunters, and "sportsmen."

96

Fur trappers took their toll of coyotes as they had been doing for decades. Even Indians had been lured into the battle in spite of their respect for or fear of the animal. When white traders offered goods or money in exchange for coyote pelts, many Navahos began killing the animals even though they believed that the ghosts of their dead resided in the bodies of coyotes. They solved that problem by first making a clay figure of a coyote for the ghost to pass into as the animal died.

Some people began to object to the incredible slaughter, but the denunciation of the predators only grew louder. Populations of hoofed animals in many areas soared to the point where they destroyed their own ranges. Forests were overbrowsed to such an extent that all of the undergrowth and much of the timber was devastated. There are scientists today who theorize that there were reasons other than predator extermination for the destructive rise in the hoofed animal populations, but the coincidence is truly remarkable.

One would hope that people learn by their mistakes and make corrections as they progress. Rather, history seems to indicate that we make excuses for our mistakes, blame something else, change a few names and theories and continue the mistakes. Now the coyote has taken the place of all the other "vicious killers" and would be the prime target for extermination if extermination were possible.

Since the initial "war," which took place in the latter part of the last century, the primary wreaker of vengeance on the coyote had been the branch of Predator and Rodent Control of the Department of the Interior. Most states had and have their own Fish and Wildlife Department. The major function of many of them is predator control.

97

As an example of their prowess in the field of killing, the federal exterminators alone reported 190,763 predators killed in the year 1970. The list included raccoons, foxes, lynxes, bobcats, badgers, wolves, bears, and mountain lions, but the greatest number killed were coyotes. The Wildlife Service workers are proud of these figures. They measure success not by how many sheep were protected, but by how many predators were killed.

In 1964 a committee was formed at the request of the Secretary of the Interior to investigate predator control to see if it was doing any good from the standpoint of agriculture and what the impact on the environment was. The result was a small document called the "Leopold Report" which stated that, in the unanimous opinion of the committee, control was "considerably in excess of the amount that can be justified in terms of total public interest."

The committee made a few recommendations among which was a basic policy change in the Predator and Rodent Control agency to reflect the broader public interest rather than simply the interests of the stockmen. It also suggested a new name for the agency, more in the line with its new policy.

Then, in 1971, the new Cain Committee on Predator Control discovered that the only basic change made by the Predator and Rodent Control agency since the Leopold Report was the selection of a new name. Now called the Division of Wildlife Services, the policies were new but the practices very much the same: control predators on the basis of "assumption of benefits rather than on proof of need," give no consideration whatever to the "positive social values of wildlife" and, simply, if there were sufficient funds to go out and kill coyotes, do it! The problem seems to be that most of the agents in the field are trappers dedicated to trapping, poisoning, and making their jobs seem necessary.

It is as though the ancient decree of the Mayan god Hunabku has come true. In a myth traced back to the Maya of Yucatán in Mexico about 1000 B.C., Hunabku, Giver of Life and Light, finds that one of his creations, people, are not multiplying. When it is reported to him that Coyote has been eating them, Hunabku demands that the culprit be brought before him. When Coyote appears, the creator asks him if he intends to continue eating people. "Yes," replies Coyote. "They're delicious."

Hunabku commands Coyote to fast for twenty days and promises that if he is successful, humans will be his only food forever. But Badger tricks Coyote into eating before the time is up, and Hunabku decrees that humans, rather than being his food, shall be his bitterest enemy. And so it has come to pass.

By far the major organized enemy of the coyote is the sheep industry. Their battle cry is, "The coyotes are putting us out of business!" in spite of the fact that what is really putting them out of business is depleted ranges and synthetic fibers that are replacing the need for wool. They distribute sarcastic bumper stickers reading, "SAVE A SHEEPMAN—TAKE A COYOTE TO LUNCH!" or, "EAT LAMB—10 MILLION COYOTES CAN'T BE WRONG!" or issue statements such as, "The lamb chops you can't afford were eaten by coyotes!" Coyotes are even accused of indirectly causing pollution and contributing to the energy crisis, although an explanation is not offered.

Perhaps the coyote has become the scapegoat for

ranchers to blame their troubles on just as Coyote was blamed for all life's little adversities by the Navahos. If there were little yellow pebbles in with the corn the women were grinding so that the meal was gritty, Coyote put them there. If there were small holes in the water jugs, Coyote had sunk his fangs into them. If the heads of the sunflowers were gone so that there were no seeds to gather, it was Coyote who had gnawed them off.

Since the general public became interested in their wildlife, and particularly since the ban on the use of poison on federal lands, the campaign of words against the coyote and other predators has increased from angry complaints to a blend of ridiculous claims and hysteria. If one listens closely the coyote grows larger and his teeth longer, his disposition becomes vicious and his numbers increase frighteningly until, as one rancher put it, stockmen will soon be herding coyotes instead of sheep.

According to one distraught sheepman, a coyote pair will increase to eight in one year, 24 the second, 70 the third, 348 the fourth and 1,597 the fifth year. Those figures are indeed alarming. At that rate our cities would soon be overrun by coyotes snapping at passers-by. But the rancher had forgotten about natural mortality. Wherever the coyote has been left alone, he and nature have kept his population stable.

During recent congressional hearings on predator control at least two witnesses, one a sheepman and the other a professor of zoology, spoke of a unique aspect of the character of the coyote. He was accused of treating livestock in an inhumane manner! Not being human, the coyote would probably agree. Coyotes that do kill livestock undoubtedly do it as coyotes do, not humans. When coyotes strike a death blow it is at least as quick and

100

merciful as the blow struck in a slaughterhouse. Coyotes almost invariably sever the jugular, unlike feral (wild) dog packs that slash at the flanks, backs or rumps of their victims.

The same two witnesses, as well as others, spoke of the immorality of not protecting domestic animals. They said that when man domesticated sheep and cattle he took away their natural ability to defend themselves and that he therefore had a moral responsibility to protect them. Animals have been domesticated for thousands of years and no one could possibly say what their behavior was like in the wild state. Even today bulls and cows are not exactly defenseless, as any coyote who has been kicked by a cow or gored by a bull would testify.

The purpose of all this strange reasoning is to convince authorities of the necessity for the use of poisons. They look on the efforts to control coyote populations as a kind of war against nature. One man stated that rats and coyotes represented the opposing forces in man's battle with nature. Others called for the use of every weapon at our disposal in that great battle against nature, and stated that control must be relentless, presumably right down to the last coyote.

Some of the weapons at our disposal are quite horrifying to anyone concerned about animal suffering. Even those who believe that predator control is necessary must cringe if they are at all knowledgeable about the effect of the weapons. The steel trap, of course, maims the foot of unwary coyotes, many of whom will chew off the offending foot in order to escape. Large numbers of "peg-leg" coyotes have been reported. Almost invariably they have become sheep killers.

But often the worst thing about the steel trap is the

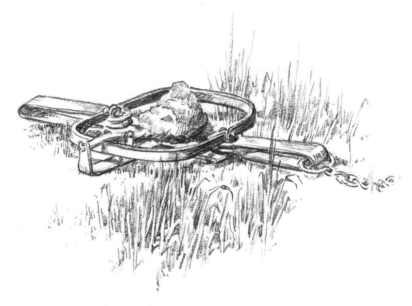

trapper. Much too often the trapline is not inspected often enough and the coyotes or other victims die slowly of starvation. Sometimes the trapped animal will be brought food by its mate, and in at least one observed case a coyote brought her trapped mate water by dunking herself so that her mate could lick the moisture from her fur. But of course that only postponed the inevitable.

There is also an ingenious device called the "Humane Coyote-Getter." It is a metal tube equipped with a spring-loaded trigger and a wad of material baited with a scent to lure the coyote. Behind the bait is a charge of cyanide. When the coyote tugs at the bait, the cyanide is shot into his mouth. It is almost one hundred percent sure death within a few minutes. Cyanide works very quickly and that is what earns the "getter" its title of "humane."

Even though the instructions clearly state that the device, now called the M-44, is "selective," meaning it is supposed to attract only coyotes, other animals do not know that. It attracts and kills any member of the dog family, including sheep dogs and the rather uncommon kit

fox, as well as skunks, raccoons, bears, the rare marten, and at least one human so far.

By far the worst of the weapons is a poison, sodium monofluoroacetate, the notorious Compound 1080. Unlike cyanide, 1080 does not decompose in bait. Any animal that eats the bait and dies becomes bait for another animal. It is more selective than strychnine or cyanide, which will kill anything, but it takes a long, excruciatingly painful time to do its deadly work. It is claimed that the poison causes a brain disconnection so that the victim does not feel the symptoms, but those who have watched the death agonies of poisoned animals believe otherwise.

How selective 1080 is depends upon how much is consumed and where the bait is put. Naturally, if baits are placed where certain animals, such as the kit fox or the marten, are not present, then the poison will be selective so far as those animals are concerned. But it is difficult to find places where there are coyotes but no skunks, raccoons, foxes, or dogs. Compound 1080 is supposed to be non-toxic to a number of animals, including humans, because their tolerance of the poison is higher than that of canines: they would have to eat more of the bait than they normally would in order to be poisoned. However, somehow the animal must be persuaded not to be a glutton. Many animals gorge themselves on occasion, particularly if they are of a species that regurgitates food for its young. Thirteen humans so far have died of 1080 poisoning.

The coyote's list of enemies does not stop with the sheepman. As long ago as 1895 the superintendent of Yellowstone National Park, where animals are supposed to be protected, recommended control of coyotes—not because they were causing harm but because they were getting too numerous! Seventy-eight years later, in the winter of 1973, a woman in the Sierra Nevada Mountains was feeding coyotes near her cabin because a heavy snowpack had reduced their food supply. Each morning and evening a man came by to shoot at them. His reason? They were "getting too friendly." There have been innumerable examples of such unreasoning prejudice directed against coyotes in the intervening years.

Hunters take a huge toll of coyotes, either specifically while looking for "varmints" to kill or incidentally while hunting other animals such as deer. The government's Division of Wildlife Services claims that hunters kill far more predators of all kinds than does the Division itself during predator control operations. There are also massive, organized coyote hunts, particularly in the plains states and in the Southwest. In a pamphlet issued by the Kansas Agricultural Experiment Station it was stated that "thousands of Kansas men and women derive a large part of their winter sport by hunting coyotes. The hunts are family or neighborhood affairs with men, women and children alike enjoying the chase. Many persons consider a coyote chase the ultimate in sport." One drive involved three thousand people who, on their happy weekend outing, killed fifty-two coyotes.

Hunting coyotes with dogs is practiced in many parts of the West, but the favorite with many was a method called "coursing," sort of a vulgar version of the British fox hunt. Trained greyhounds or wolfhounds were packed into a vehicle and then bounced across the plains until a coyote was spotted. Then the hounds were released to catch the coyote and tear it to pieces. Even though the coyote is considered the fastest of all wild canines, it is apparently no match for hounds bred for speed and racing.

As Leon Almirall describes this "sport" in his book of 1941, *Canines and Coyotes*, "Fights to the finish were such as to send thrills through anyone who likes to hunt where the sporting chance exists. Where no sporting chances exist, neither do good sportsmen." The "good sportsman" does not mention how the coyote has a sporting chance against three or four hounds that can outrun him and that are almost twice his size.

There are also the varmint callers who use a device that can be made to sound like the distress call of a rabbit, thus enabling them to lure a coyote to within shooting distance. Others, who seem to prefer a more direct contact with the chase and the killing, enjoy roping the coyote from a horse and then finishing it off with a club or bullet. Still others delight in chasing coyotes in jeeps across the fields and running them down. With the advent of the snowmobile a great new winter sport was invented: using the machine to run down coyotes or any other animal that cannot run very well in deep snow.

It is interesting that the "sportsmen" just described

105

frequently refer to coyotes as vicious killers or murderers. Almirall in another part of his book says of a coyote dying from wounds administered by the hounds and a clout on the head, " . . . his hard, cold eyes glaze with a dying hatred. Another small-game murderer has gone on his way out."

The reasons for this slaughter are varied. Some people seem to think that wildlife has been provided for their amusement, and they are somehow entertained by killing animals. Others act out of prejudice, the source of which they would find difficult or impossible to trace.

A good example of mindless reaction against coyotes occurred recently in Maine. A coyote had been shot and hung up in a town square for people to see, since the animal is quite rare in the Northeast. Among those who came to see the hanging were many who cursed and spit on the carcass, as though trying to cast out evil spirits.

A few westerners even have an insane hatred for coyotes, such as the men who take live coyotes from traps and hang them from fences to die of starvation, or the man who wired a coyote's jaw shut and turned it loose, or another man who delighted in sawing off a coyote's lower jaw and turning him loose with the dogs. Perhaps many are influenced by childhood stories about the *thieving* raccoon, the *sneaky* fox, the *cowardly* coyote and, of course, the big, *bad* wolf.

Or perhaps they have heard and believed stories of "killing orgies" attributed to canine predators, going back to medieval European tales of packs of wolves attacking and carrying off villagers. There has never been a proven case of humans being attacked by wolves, let alone coyotes, unless the animals were rabid. Most of the "killing orgies" involving livestock have been traced to dogs gone

tion. At Isle Royale National Park in Lake Superior, where protected wolves maintain a natural balance with moose, coyotes once ruled. But when the wolves moved in about fifty years ago, all the coyotes mysteriously disappeared.

Occasionally a coyote might run afoul of a cougar or a bear, usually because of the coyote's hunger overcoming his caution. Normally bears or cougars do not attack coyotes unless they try to move in on a fresh kill. But the coyote's usual attitude is patience. Hungry coyotes have been known to wait as long as four days by a kill deserted by a cougar before daring to approach the carcass.

In Indian myths Coyote had few enemies but many did get angry with him, such as the rattlesnake the Omaha Indians of the southern plains told about. One day Coyote was trotting in a straight line across the prairie when he heard someone say, "Stop!" He looked all around but could see no one so he took a few more steps. Then someone said, "Walk around me!"

Coyote looked down, saw Rattlesnake and said, "Hmph! When I walk here I don't want to walk around anybody. You get out of my way!"

"I am here! I never give way to anyone," said Rattlesnake.

"Then I will run over you," said Coyote.

"If you do," said Rattlesnake, "you shall die."

"Why should I die?" asked Coyote. "There is nothing that can kill me."

"Step over me, then," said Rattlesnake. "Do it in spite of me."

Coyote stepped over him and Rattlesnake bit him, but he did not feel it.

"Where is it?" asked Coyote laughingly. "Where have I received my death blow?"

Rattlesnake said nothing and Coyote went on. Soon he

109

came to a creek. As he was about to drink, he saw himself in the water.

"I am very fat," he said to himself. "I was not fat before."

He felt himself all over. He was indeed very fat and swollen. But he walked on until he felt very sleepy. He lay down and went to sleep. He never woke up. Rattlesnake had spoken the truth.

The Paiute Indians told about a flock of snow geese that once landed in the Great Basin country of the Paiute near where Coyote lay resting. Coyote wanted to go with the geese and made a nuisance of himself. The geese considered him a pest but finally fitted him out by sticking feathers in his fur. Then they all took off for the south with Coyote flapping among them. But once they were airborne the geese pulled out all of Coyote's feathers and Coyote fell to his death.

But Coyote can never really die. As the Navaho say, he keeps his life forces in the tip of his nose and the tip of his tail. When his body is killed he simply pulls his life forces together and comes to life. Friends of the coyote who do not count on that must remember that the coyote's human enemies live, work, and play where the coyotes are and that most of those on the side of the animal are in the cities. Although the latter may well be in the majority, they still will have to do a lot of howling to protect their friends.

8 · Justice for the Coyote

An ecosystem is a community of living and non-living things. It is the trees, shrubs, herbs, grasses, mosses, algae, and fungi of the plant kingdom. It is the insects, arachnids, mollusks, fish, reptiles, amphibians, birds, mammals and hundreds of other organisms and micro-organisms of the animal kingdom. And it is the soil, minerals, rocks, and air that make the life of plants and animals possible.

The community can be as tiny a world as certain species of algae and fungi that combine to form ecosystems called lichens. Or it can be as large as an ecosystem called the planet Earth. The complexity of even a small ecosystem is sufficient to stagger the mind.

Ecology is the study of the relationship between these living and non-living things—that relationship which maintains the balance of nature. Ecology is a relatively new science and scientists have yet but little understanding of even the smaller ecosystems. What scientists have learned and do understand is just now beginning to make a small impression on the general public.

Coyotes, of course, are members of various ecosystems throughout a large part of our continent. They are by far the most numerous of our large predators. They are certainly the most economically important to man of all the large wild animals, if for no other reason than that large sums of money are spent trying to control or eradicate the animals. Yet very little is known about coyotes, let alone the ecosystem of which they are a part. Studies in ecology have largely ignored them. Studies in autecology, concerning the relationship of *one* species to its environment, have ignored them. And studies in ethology, concerning animal behavior, have ignored them.

The question reasonably has been asked why so many millions have been spent in an attempt to eliminate a species of animal so little is known about, particularly when there is no indication that its extermination would be a benefit to anyone, including its enemies. The Cain Report made a hearty recommendation that considerable research be done on predators and especially on coyotes in the wild. It seems a much better plan than to kill first and ask questions later.

The U. S. Bureau of Sport Fisheries and Wildlife consists of numerous divisions, one of which devotes its time to research and another of which, the Division of Wildlife Services, devotes most of its time to killing animals, particularly coyotes. Somehow the results of the research division's studies always seem to indicate to the Division of Wildlife Services that more and more coyotes must be killed. But the studies are really of methods of predator control rather than of the ecology of the coyote. The coyote will have to look elsewhere for justice.

Oddly enough, he gets a measure of protection in areas where he could least expect it. A number of cattle ranches have posted NO COYOTE HUNTING signs. The owners have come to realize that the coyote is their friend. Some years ago a group of ranchers in Colorado formed an association to protect coyotes and other predators on their lands. They had found that when the predators had been almost eliminated, the increasing rodent populations threatened to destroy their ranges.

In one state a near range war developed between cattlemen trying to protect coyotes and sheepmen trying to kill them. Throughout the West a few individual ranchers have persisted in protecting coyotes even though losing friends and making enemies as a result. One enormous ranch which operates a 400,000 acre spread on the Wyoming-Montana border issues permits to people who wish to hunt deer and pronghorn antelope on its lands. The permits, specifically prohibiting the shooting of coyotes, are signed by J. B. Kendrick. The attitude toward coyotes has changed considerably since Senator J. B. Kendrick made the speech quoted in Chapter Seven.

A number of ranchers have urged that their peers would be much better off if they would learn to live with coyotes. That would seem to be an enlightened and logical suggestion since coyotes certainly seem to be here to stay. But there is no question that *some* coyotes eat *some* of the

sheep of *some* of the ranchers. How do those ranchers learn to live with coyotes?

There is no way to persuade a sheepman to share his sheep with a coyote who prefers mutton for dinner. The answer is to eliminate those coyotes who develop the wrong food habits, not the entire population. After years of attempts to control coyote populations it should be apparent that it cannot be done. Kansas and Missouri have long operated under a system where only the individuals responsible for killing sheep are sought. Ranchers are taught by the Wildlife Damage Control Department of the University of Kansas how to trap, or hunters are brought in to eliminate the offenders. Poisons are not used,

since even if they could be proved to be safe and selective, there is no way to control the man who dispenses the poisons.

New traps have been developed which are constructed so that the jaws do not completely close yet are strong enough to hold a coyote without breaking its foot. Some of the traps are padded so that not even the skin is bruised. A. Starker Leopold and his students recently tested a new type of trap in California and caught some of the animals sixteen times without hurting them. It might be said that they were either particularly dumb coyotes or they got a free snack each time they were caught.

Numerous other methods of coyote control are being tested. From the standpoint of humaneness and the environment, all are probably much better than poison, but from the coyotes' standpoint some must be just as objectionable. Certain of the proposed biological controls are enough to make a coyote's fur stand on end. The most radical of such methods is to change the environment to make it unsuitable for the predator. Since the coyote is so adaptable this would seem to be impossible, unless the environment were changed sufficiently to make it unsuitable for anything, including humans.

A method getting serious attention is the use of chemosterilants—chemical agents that render the animal sterile. Since there is no pain or death involved, coyotes would have no way to learn to avoid the substance. This learning process, which has been noted through the coyotes' contact with baited carcasses and Coyote-Getters, is called "aversive conditioning." The problem yet to be solved is to find a bait that will attract only coyotes. Work is being done to isolate pheromones to use for bait which would be appealing to coyotes. Pheromones are hormonal secretions from an animal that cause a physiological or behavioral response from animals of the same species.

But chemosterilants could only be used in population control, not against individual marauding animals. So far the effect of the sterility agents are temporary. If they are made to have a permanent effect and are used in massive doses they could easily exterminate the species.

Other chemicals that have been tried are antifertility agents. A test was made in two large areas in New Mexico where antifertility baits were dropped in one area while the other area was kept unbaited. After sufficient time, coyotes were collected from the two areas. All thirteen coyotes taken from the unbaited area were pregnant, but sixteen out of the twenty taken from the baited area had had pregnancies blocked.

The Bureau of Sport Fisheries and Wildlife is investigating other chemicals that a reasonable coyote might consider more just. Experiments using compounds that cause diarrhea or nausea or that have a repelling odor have been made. The problem, of course, is how to get the coyote to "take the pill" under the right conditions so that he will learn to avoid it in the future. One idea is the use of a collar with a pouch containing the compound around the necks of all the lambs of a flock. The pouch would be placed over the jugular vein, which the coyote almost invariably attacks. Theoretically, by the time the rancher lost a lamb or two the coyote would be aversively conditioned.

The method of deterring coyotes from bothering sheep that would get a canine stamp of approval is the spraying of an entire grazing area with cheap perfume by aircraft. This idea was investigated after it was discovered that cheap perfume makes coyotes sick. Of course it might make sheep sick, too.

The beginning of significant justice for the coyote and other predators came when former President Nixon issued an executive order banning the use of all poisons for predator or rodent control if they have a secondary effect—that is, if they are passed along the food chain from animal to animal.

But much more justice is needed for the coyote. If our natural heritages are to be protected, the people who "manage" the wilds and wildlife must at least be trained scientists with a thorough understanding of ecology. They must also understand that, as the Leopold Report of 1964 stated, "for every person whose sheep may be molested by a coyote there are perhaps a thousand others who would thrill to hear a coyote chorus in the night," and that, as the Cain Report stated seven years later, "As society grows in environmental awareness, it increasingly cherishes the full variety of a natural environment. This certainly includes coyotes and other predators. The right of any limited segment of society to reduce or eliminate predators is increasingly open to question."

Some say there is a need for a method of reimbursing that limited segment of society, the ranchers who raise

117

livestock, for their losses to coyotes. The unfortunate alternative may be that the stockmen will take matters into their own hands by poisoning illegally, without professional help or knowledge. Some already have used black-market poisons from Mexico. This action has been threatened by proponents of poison for over forty years whenever someone wants to take their poisons away.

Many persons knowledgeable about both the plight of the coyote and about predations against sheep recommend a kind of insurance program. Another possibility is to create a federal subsidy to pay stockmen for their losses to coyotes. This is based on the reasoning that since coyotes do belong to the people of the United States, the people should help pay for losses caused by coyotes. A recent counterargument is that coyotes are residents of the various states and therefore are the states' responsibility.

In fact, of course, coyotes belong to the environment and it is part of the business of ranching to contend with the components of that environment. Sheep themselves are destructive of the ranges upon which they graze, since they have a tendency to gouge the grass out of the ground rather than clip it as do cattle and horses. John Muir called sheep "hooved locusts" and almost one hundred years ago led a fight to get them off public lands. The question still remains: why are such destructive animals still allowed on lands belonging to all the people? But it is adding insult to injury to demand the destruction of animals *native* to the ranges.

There is considerably more that sheepmen can do to protect their flocks and bands from coyotes before resorting to poison or even biological or non-toxic chemical controls. Many, if not most, sheepmen no longer herd their sheep, saying either that it is too expensive or that they cannot get good shepherds. Studies have shown that tended flocks suffer from predation far less than do those that are untended. The savings in uneaten sheep might provide funds for training and paying for good shepherds.

But perhaps the greatest need of all is for a new ethic, an environmental ethic—a new set of values regarding nature. We have now come to that point in time when we, as a species, can do little without affecting the environment. There are just too many of us and of our machines. The state of our technology is more advanced than that of our wisdom. We now even have sufficient knowledge, and probably will soon have the ability, to alter genes and thus change the natural course of evolution. It is a frightening prospect, considering the moral state of the species that is capable of developing and using nuclear weapons.

Thus, many scientists are pointing out that there is an urgent need for what some call "evolutionary ethics"—a code of conduct to guide human beings, not only in their relations with each other but also in relationship to the total environment, so that we may be morally prepared for that day when we learn how to alter genes, change the weather, dominate space, create earthquakes, rejuvenate ancient volcanoes, melt the ice caps. Whatever humans learn how to do, sooner or later they do, regardless of the consequences.

Our record has not been good. We have created vast deserts where there were once forests and grasslands; we have exterminated or decimated entire species of plants and animals; we have befouled the air we breathe and the water we drink; we have planned our cities to suit our machines first and ourselves second. It is only quite

119

recently, in the past sixty or seventy years at the most, that we have even become aware of the need for the conservation of resources, and perhaps only in the last twenty years that we have seen the need for environmentalism—a concern for the environment as a whole rather than just for specific resources.

It is said that this is the era of environmental awareness. How we treat coyotes can be an indication of the extent of that awareness and can also have a direct bearing on how we treat one another. If we tolerate the attempt to exterminate a species of animal, such callousness can carry over in our attitude toward other animals, people, and entire ecosystems, as it has in the past.

On the other hand, if we come to understand the rightful place of the coyote, or any other animal, in our communal environment, to understand that its ecological niche fulfills the needs of that environment and therefore fulfills our needs also, then we may gain a better understanding of our own ecological niche. We have not understood this and generally do not yet understand it.

Seventy years ago Ernest Thompson Seton made an appeal to the younger generation of his time. "My chief motive . . . has been to stop the extermination of harmless wild animals; not for their sake but for ours, firmly believing that each of our wild creatures is in itself a precious heritage that we have no right to destroy or put beyond the reach of our children. I have tried to stop the stupid and brutal work of destruction by an appeal—not to reason; that has failed hitherto—but to sympathy, and especially the sympathies of the younger generation."

Again it is to young people that the appeal is made. While scientists argue the abstractions of ethical conduct

120

toward the environment, the young must battle in the field. The battle will be won, not by arguments and documents, but by demands from the people. The older generation, with few exceptions, is still basically committed to the value system wherein everything must serve the interests of man.

The philosophers and scientists can, of course, formulate and plead for any number of codes of environmental ethics. Scientists historically have been moral people whose ideas, creations, and inventions have too often been utilized by moral idiots. But if the values continue to be the old ones of growth, "progress," and exploitation at any cost, then the codes will remain idealistic theories that are referred to from time to time like well-loved poems—sources of inspiration but not spurs to action.

If a code is not established and accepted by the people of the world, then it is possible that human beings, in attempting to reap the harvest without considering the limits of the planet's resources and in attempting to eliminate whatever species of plant or animal they consider without value to them or in competition with them, may well create an environment to which humans themselves cannot adapt.

It is difficult for people to think of themselves as anything less than the most important creatures on earth. As a species, we are only one of many of equal importance to the environment, but our demands continue to increase out of all proportion to our worth. Because of our unreasonable demands upon nature, we may become as expendable as the dinosaur, now vanished from the face of the earth.

121

The coyote makes few demands. When they become unreasonable, some coyotes perish, the demands are lessened, and other coyotes prosper and sniff the man-torn world, seeking new places in which to wander.

"My world," sang the coyote of the Maidu Indians of California, "where one travels by the valley edge,

"My world of foggy mountains
Where one goes meandering
Here and there, range after range
I sing of the country I shall travel in
In such a world I shall wander."

The coyote is secure. The Indians have said, "Coyote cannot die."

Index

123

ABOUT THE AUTHOR
Harold E. Thomas gave up a career in technical publications to turn cattleman and farmer. He now runs a rare plant nursery in the foothills of the Sierra Nevada Mountains near Clovis, California. Conservation chairman of his local chapter of the Sierra Club, he is also a member of Defenders of Wildlife and Friends of the Earth.

ABOUT THE ILLUSTRATOR
Lorence F. Bjorklund, a graduate of Pratt Institute, has illustrated more than three hundred and fifty books, mostly on western subjects, and has written and illustrated books on animals and Indians. Originally from Minnesota, he lives in Croton Falls, New York, and summers in Maine.